SPICE IT UP

Recipes
with a
Sensual Twist

by LaJuan Preston

RoseDog 🐾 Books

PITTSBURGH, PENNSYLVANIA 15238

RoseDog Books
585 Alpha Drive
Pittsburgh, PA 15238
Visit our website at *www.dorrancebookstore.com*

ISBN: 978-1-4809-8814-9
eISBN: 978-1-4809-8182-9

This book is dedicated to my grandparents Rosa & Hubert Johnson. Without them I would not have the knowledge on cooking, & recipes. May you both rest in heavenly peace. I love and miss you both.

Acknowledgements

I would like to give thanks to GOD for the guidance and direction that I pray for every day.

Jordan & Eric Howell, my sons, thank you for allowing me to use you two as testers on my recipes over the years and giving me your honest opinions. I'm really proud of both of you. I love you both.

Patricia Lee, thank you for raising us with values and morals. Mom, you're the best, I love you.

Renager Lee, thank you for being there for mom, and giving us advice when we need it.

Douglas Preston, Michelle Preston (RIP), Robin Scott, & Marcus Warfield, thank you for being the best brothers and sisters that a person could ask for. Always remember that you can achieve anything if you put your mind to it. I Love you all.

Karen Warfield, you never treated me like an outsider. You always treated me and talked to me with kindness and respect. I love you.

Leslie Jenkins, and Kelli Bacon, Thanks for coming to me for advice and letting me be a part of your lives. Love you much.

Barbara Johnson, Gary Lee, Mavis Taylor, Thanks for your support and prayers.

David Tinsley, Graylin Howell and Rodney Hilton, Thanks for all the support and advice you have given me over the years, showing me how much you LOVE me, giving me the guidance, direction and confidence to go after my dream and most importantly being my friend.

La Faye Short, Thanks for the contribution of recipes and being a sister to me since we moved to Alexandria. I Love you.

Wendell Weathers, thank you for the music you provided for Spice It Up! With La Juan, the pilot I shot for the TV show.

My co-workers at US Airways, now the New American Airlines, thanks for all your support you have given me. FLY SAFE!!!!!!

Toni Worrell, you have truly been a blessing to me over the years. You are a huge inspiration to me. I am so thankful and grateful you are in my life.

Monique Vaughn, Sharon Reyes, Katherine Clark, Doris Fudo, Deanna Rutherford, Sonja Weathers, Sabrina McClain, Sheila Bannister, Doris Coleman (RIP), Priscilla Jones, Pamela Mangum, Sheneal Norville, you all are my sisters. Thank you for your encouragement and support over the years. I Love You.

Charlotte Fire Department (Station #16 C Shift, Station 26, A& B shift, station 37 C shift, Station 32 C shift) thanks for giving me the opportunity to cook some of my recipes for you.

Robb Ferguson, thank you for giving me my first commercial catering job.

To those of you who have helped me, who have supported me but wish to remain anonymous or those of you that I work beside often. You know who you are. Thank you very much.

Introduction

This book was written to give those who don't know how to cook, the opportunity to cook a meal and also put a little fun and spice in the relationship at the same time. These are very easy recipes to follow.

As you will discover in this book, you will not only find recipes for cooking, but also helpful tips on keeping the spice not only in your food but in your relationship.

Everyone wants a little excitement in their lives. What better way to enhance the excitement by cooking, and making love to your partner both physically, and mentally.

This book in tells ways of pleasing your partner through his/her palate, as well as places and things to do to make love to your partner physically and to his/her mind. Chemistry plays a big part in cooking and relationships. This book was designed to cook with your partner in and out of the kitchen. This book helps to put and keep some chemistry and **spice in your relationship**.

At the end of each chapter there will be blank pages for you to keep little notes, to write in your favorite recipe, or just list certain recipes or tips that you found helpful.

I invite and encourage you to try some of the recipes in and out of the kitchen and **SPICE IT UP!!**

Glossary

Al dente

Pasta cooked on the outside and firm on the inside.

Bake

Cook using dry heat in an oven.

Baste

Moisten food using drippings from pan during cooking.

Blend

Mix 2 or more ingredients by hand, blender or mixer.

Boil

To bring up to a temperature that you see rolling bubbles breaking the surface.

Brown

Cook with a little oil to bring outer meat to the color brown. Do not cook all the way through usually on a med high heat.

Chop

Cut into small pieces

Coat

Cover food with flour, bread crumbs, egg mixture, batter, or chocolate.

Cordial

Alcoholic Liquor (liqueur)

Cream

Soften, or combine one or more ingredients together.

Deglazing

A liquid usually wine or stock is used after you brown the meat, and the meat is removed. Scrape the bottom of the pan with a wooden spoon.

Fold

Combine a delicate mixture to a heavier mixture without a loss of air.

Fry

To cook in about ½ - 1 cup oil.

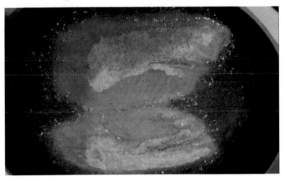

Hors D'oeuvre

Small serving portions, usually appetizers.

Marinating

Soak meat in liquid or dry rub for a period of time usually from 20 minutes to overnight.

Mince

Cut into very small pieces.

Pre Heat

Turn on the appliance to heat up before cooking.

Roast

To cook uncovered in the oven.

Simmer

Cook in liquid on low heat below boiling point. You will see tiny bubbles.

Slice

Cut into uniform pieces.

Stew

Simmer long and slow in liquid in a covered pot.

Stir

Mix ingredients using a circular motion.

Toss

Using a lifting motion, tumble ingredients

36-24-36

ABBREVIATIONS

C. = Cup

Oz. = Ounce

Tbsp. = Tablespoon

tsp. = Teaspoon

Lbs. = Pound

Pt. = Pint

Qt= Quart

Gal= Gallon

MEASUREMENTS

3 teaspoons = 1 Tbsp.

2 Tablespoons = 1 ounce

1 teaspoon = 1 ml

1 Tablespoon = 15 ml

1 cup = 8 oz.

2 c = 1 pt or ½ Qt.

2 pt = 1 Qt.

4 Qt. = 1 Gal.

8 c = ½ Gal.

1 c = 16 Tbsp.

¾ c =12 Tbsp.

½ c = 8 Tbsp.

¼ c = 4 Tbsp.

1/3 c = 6 Tbsp.

2/3 c = 10 Tbsp.

WEIGHT

1 lb. bread flour (sifted) = 4 cups

1 lb. of cake flour = 4 ¼ cups

1 lb. sugar = 2 ¼ cups

4 eggs = 1 cup

MEAT TEMPERATURE

Poultry 185 degrees (whole)

Pork, Lamb, Beef (well done) 180 degrees

Poultry Breast 170 degrees

Fresh Ham, Veal, Lamb, Pork, Beef 160 degrees

Cooked Ham 160 degrees

Beef (Rare) 140 degrees

DISTILLED SPIRITS

50 ML Miniature

200 ML ½ pt.

500 ML 1 pt.

750 ML 4.5 quart

1 Liter 1 Quart

1.75 Liter ½ Gallon

Contents

CHAPTER 1

COCK-TAILS & FORE-PLAY
(Drinks & Appetizers)

Angel Face

Apples with Brandy Cinnamon

Baked Crab Dip

Breast Caresser

Chocolate Bars

Crab Cakes

Eggnog

Hot Chocolate

Kiss

Lemon Lime Punch

Oysters Casino

Purple Passion

Salmon Pate'

Sloe Screw

Spinach Balls

Spinach Dip

Trail Mix

Apple Punch

Bahama Mama Punch

Brandied Apple

Caramel Corn with Nuts

Clam Dip

Drunk Nuts

Fruit Punch

Iced Tea

Mixed Fruit Smoothie

Mint Julep

Peppermint Schnapps

Ranch Mix

Sausage Balls

Spicy Warm Nuts

Spinach Ball Sauce

Sub Sandwich

Tropical Fruit Drink

ANGEL FACE

1 shot Gin
½ shot Apricot Brandy
½ shot Apple Brandy

Shake well with ice and strain into a cocktail glass.

APPLE PUNCH

1 ½ quarts Apple juice
2 Cinnamon sticks
8 whole cloves
1 1/3 cup Pineapple juice
½ cup Lemon juice
2 pints Orange juice
1 liter Ginger ale

Place Apple juice in a non-aluminum pot; tie spices in cheesecloth, add to pot, and simmer uncovered for 15 minutes; discard spice bag. Mix spiced juice with remaining fruit juices. To serve, place a large block of ice in a large punch bowl, add fruit juice and ginger ale.

> ***Tip: To make ice block: Freeze some orange juice in a whipped topping container with lid. ***

APPLES WITH BRANDY CINNAMON

1 stick Butter
1 c. Brandy
4 c. Apples
1 ¼ c. Sugar
2 Tbsp. Lemon juice
2 tsp. Vanilla
1 ½ tsp. Cinnamon

Over a medium heat, melt butter, add brandy, apples, sugar, and cinnamon. Stir well, add vanilla and lemon juice. Turn down to low and simmer until apples are soft.

BAHAMA MAMA PUNCH

½ oz. Dark rum
½ oz. 151 proof Rum
½ oz. Coconut liqueur
½ oz. Coffee liqueur
4 oz. Pineapple juice
½ Lemon, juiced

Stir all ingredients with ice and strain into a chilled glass filled with ice. Garnish with a cherry or a slice of pineapple.

BAKED CRAB DIP

1 package (8 oz) cream cheese, softened
1 can (6 oz) crabmeat
2 Tbsp. grated onion
1 Tbsp. milk
1/2 tsp. salt
1/4 tsp. pepper
1/4 tsp. Worcestershire sauce
1 tsp. Hot Sauce
1 Tbsp. finely sliced green onions, for garnish

In a bowl, combine cream cheese, crabmeat, onion, hot sauce, milk, salt & pepper, and Worcestershire sauce. Mix well. Place mixture in an small oven-proof serving dish. Bake @ 375 degrees for 15 minutes, or until thoroughly heated. Sprinkle with sliced green onion.

BRANDIED APPLE

2 shots of E & J Brandy
Apple Juice

In a glass, fill with ice. Add brandy and top off with apple juice. Stir well.

BREAST CARESSER

1 shot brandy
1 shot Madeira
½ shot triple sec

Stir with ice and strain. Serve in Martini Glass.

CARAMEL CORN WITH NUTS

8 cups popcorn, popped
2 cups Spanish peanuts (or your favorite nut)
¾ cup firmly packed brown sugar
6 Tbsp. butter
3 Tbsp. light corn syrup
¼ tsp. baking soda
¼ tsp. vanilla
¼ tsp. salt
1 cup pecan halves

Preheat your oven to 300 degrees. Remove all kernels that did not pop. Put popcorn pecan halves, & peanuts onto a large cookie sheet. In a saucepan combine sugar, butter, corn syrup, and salt. Cook and stir over medium heat until butter melts and mixture come to a boil. Cook, for 5 minutes more, **DO NOT STIR**, remove from heat. Stir in baking soda and vanilla. Pour over popcorn; gently fold to coat popcorn and nuts. Bake in oven for 15 minutes & stir. Bake an extra 5 -10 minutes. Put popcorn to a large bowl & cool.

CHOCOLATE BARS

1 ½ c. finely crushed thin pretzels
1 ½ sticks butter or margarine, melted
1 -14 oz can Sweetened condensed milk (<u>NOT evaporated milk</u>)
4 bars (4 oz) Unsweetened Baking Chocolate, broken into pieces
2 c. mini marshmallows
1 c. Sweetened Coconut Flakes
1 c. coarsely chopped pecans or pecan pieces
4 bars (4 oz) Semi-Sweet Baking Chocolate, broken into pieces
1 Tbsp. shortening

Preheat oven to 350 degrees. Combine pretzels and melted butter in small bowl; press evenly into bottom of 9x13-inch baking pan. Place sweetened condensed milk and unsweetened chocolate in small microwave-safe bowl. Microwave at HIGH 1 to 1 1/2 minutes. Mixture should be melted and smooth when stirred. Pour over pretzel layer in pan. Top with marshmallows, coconut and pecans; press firmly down onto chocolate layer. Bake 25 to 30 minutes or until lightly browned; cool completely in pan on a wire rack. Melt semi-sweet chocolate and shortening in small microwave-safe bowl at HIGH for 45 seconds to 1 minute or until melted when stirred; drizzle over entire top. Refrigerate 30 minutes. Cut into bars.

CLAM DIP

1 lb. bacon, cooked, drained and minced

1 Tbsp. horseradish

2 oz. Sour cream

1/3 cup mayonnaise

2 hardboiled egg (chopped)

1 tsp. mustard

2 small can clams, chopped, drained

½ tsp. parsley (fresh)

1 small container French Onion Dip

Blend together all ingredients. Cover and refrigerate for at least 1 hour before serving.

CRAB CAKES

½ tsp. garlic minced

1 Tbsp. onion minced

1 Tbsp. celery diced

2 Tbsp. mayonnaise

1 whole egg (beaten)

1/8 tsp. salt

1/8 tsp. black pepper

1 tsp. Dijon mustard

1 tsp. Cajun seasoning

1 tsp. Old Bay

¼ cup bread crumbs

1 lb. lump crab meat

2 Tbsp. oil for sautéing

In a large bowl, combine all ingredients except crab meat and bread crumbs. Using gloved hands, gently mix in crab meat, and then add bread crumbs. Spread a thin layer of plain bread crumbs on work surface. Form crab mixture into equal balls, approximately 2" in diameter. Place on crumbs. Gently flatten ball of crab mixture and round the edges to form cakes about 1/2" thick and 3" round. Refrigerate for 1 hour. In a sauté pan, melt 2 tablespoons of oil until hot. Gently slide in crab cakes 2 at a time. Cook for 3 minutes on this side. Turn and brown on the other side for 3 minutes. Turn down heat to simmer and cook crab cakes another 5 - 8 minutes, or bake at 350 for 10 minutes.

DRUNK NUTS

3 Tbsp. butter, melted
2 cups Pecans, whole or halves
2 Tbsp. Bourbon

Melt the butter in a skillet. Toss in the pecans and stir until glazed (over a low flame). Add the bourbon and continue to heat until most of the liquid has evaporated. Lay nuts out on a sheet of wax paper to cool. Cover and store at room temperature until ready to eat.

EGGNOG

2 cups sugar
1 dozen eggs separated
1- 1 ½ c. Dark Rum
1- 1 ½ c. Bourbon
9 egg whites
1/2 tsp. salt
6 ½ c. Heavy Whipping Cream
2 ½ Tbsp. Vanilla extract
Dash of nutmeg
½ cup of whip cream (heavy) for topping (optional)

Beat eggs and sugar until thick. Continue beating, adding rum and whiskey.

Refrigerate for 4 hours. While mixture is chilling, beat egg whites and salt together until you have soft peaks. In a separate bowl, beat cream until stiff. Pour chilling mixture in a Punch bowl fold in whipped cream then fold in egg whites. Chill for 1 to 2 hours. You may add additional liquor if not strong enough. Sprinkle with nutmeg before serving.

FRUIT PUNCH

3 cups Instant pink lemonade
2 ½ cups pineapple juice
2 cups white grape juice
2 ½ cups water
1 cup gin or vodka (optional)
Use a large glass or plastic pitcher. Add juices & water. Stir until drink mix is dissolved. Serve over ice.

HOT CHOCOLATE

3 cups Half & Half
1/4 cup unsweetened cocoa ½ cup instant chocolate drink mix.
1 1/2 tsp. Vanilla Extract
1/8 tsp. salt
6 cups hot water
Mini Marshmallows or whipped cream (optional)

In a large saucepan, combine half & half milk, chocolate drink mix, cocoa, vanilla and salt; mix well. Over medium heat, slowly stir in water; heat through, stirring occasionally. **DO NOT BOIL**. Top with marshmallows or whipped cream, if desired.

ICED TEA

8 of your favorite brand tea bags
1 3/4 cups sugar
1 gallon water
1 small can concentrated lemonade (optional)

Place tea bags in a pot. Add only enough water to cover bags, about ½ gallon, bring to a boil. Drain tea bags and add sugar. Add to ½ gallon water - stir in lemonade and chill. If you want tea stronger, let tea bags steep for a time in the refrigerator.

> ***TIP: This tea can be also made as sun tea. Place in a jar and set in the sun.

KISS

1 shot Gin
1 shot Cherry Brandy
1 shot Dry Vermouth
1 shot Viniq Cocktail

Stir and pour over ice.
(Pucker Up)

LEMON LIME PUNCH

2 qt Cold water
2 c. Lemon Lime soda (sprite, twist or 7 up)
½ c. Lemon juice
½ c. Lime juice
1 pt. Lime sherbet

In a pitcher mix first four ingredients. In each glass place a scoop of sherbet and punch.

MINT JULEP

1 ½ tsp. Powdered Sugar
2 oz. Brandy (1 ½ shot)
1 shot Peach Schnapps
3 sprigs Mint leaves
1 ½ shot Bourbon

Place ice and mint leaves into a glass. Add powdered sugar with a splash of water to dissolve sugar a little. Add brandy, bourbon, and peach schnapps. Stir.

MIXED FRUIT SMOOTHIE

1 cup non-fat plain yogurt
1 cup soy milk (vanilla)
1 cup Pineapple juice
1 cup frozen mixed fruit
12 ice cubes

Put all ingredients in to a blender. Blend until smooth. Pour into a large glass.

OYSTERS CASINO

12 large oysters

6 slices bacon

½ cup finely chopped onion

¼ cup finely chopped celery

¼ cup finely chopped green pepper

2 teaspoons lemon juice

½ teaspoon salt

1 teaspoon Worcestershire sauce

4 to 6 drops Tabasco

If your oysters are not in a shell, place oysters on a baking dish. If they are in a shell, shuck the oysters, discarding any liquid. Save the shell, wash and dry the oyster shells. Set aside. Preheat oven to 375 degrees. In a skillet fry bacon until partially cooked. Add onion, celery, and green pepper and cook until tender. Add lemon juice, salt, Worcestershire sauce and Tabasco. Arrange oysters either in or out of their shells and place on a baking sheet. Divide bacon mixture evenly over oysters. Bake in a 375 degree oven for 10 to 12 minutes or until edges of oysters begin to curl and topping is brown.

PEPPERMINT SCHNAPPS

½ c. granulated sugar

4 cups white corn syrup

4 cups Vodka

4 teaspoon Peppermint extract

Heat the corn syrup in a saucepan. Whisk in the sugar. Heat until sugar is dissolved. Stirring for five minutes. Remove from the heat. Whisk in the vodka. Cover and cool at room temperature. Whisk in the peppermint extract. Place in a bottle and seal. Chill well before serving (optional).

PURPLE PASSION

4 oz. Grape juice
4 oz. Grapefruit juice
1 ½ shot Vodka
1 shot Viniq Cocktail
Sugar to taste (optional)

Stir and Pour over ice.

RANCH MIX

1 envelope Ranch salad dressing
2 tablespoons dried dill weed
6 cups cereal, corn and rice (3 each)
1 10-ounce package oyster crackers, or Ritz Bits
1 6-ounce package pretzel sticks
¾ cup vegetable oil

Combine dressing mix and dill weed; add cereal, crackers, and pretzels. Combine well. Drizzle mixture with oil; stir to coat thoroughly. Place mixture in a large paper bag; let stand for about 2 hours, shaking occasionally. This can be stored in an airtight container.

SALMON PATE

Pictured is what the Salmon Pate is supposed to look like before you add the spices and cream cheese and form it into a ball.

2 cans Pink Salmon (drained, skinned and crumbled)
8 oz. Cream cheese (softened)
1 Tbsp. Seasoning Blend
1 Tbsp. Season Salt
1 tsp. Garlic Powder
1 Lemon juiced
8 dashes of Hot Sauce

In a large bowl mix all ingredients together. Form into a ball in the middle of a plate or platter. Slice 2 thin slices of lemon, form parsley sprigs around the base of the ball. Sprinkle with Paprika and garnish with lemon slices on top.

SAUSAGE BALLS

2 roll Sausage (or your favorite breakfast sausage) (I prefer hot)
2 cup of shredded cheddar cheese

1 Tbsp. Crushed red pepper flakes

½ tsp. Garlic powder

1 cup Bisquick

Mix ingredients together in large bowl. Roll into small balls about 1 inch, place on a very lightly greased cookie sheet. Bake at 375 degrees until brown.

SLOE SCREW

2 shots Sloe Gin

½ shot Vodka

Orange Juice

Pour the sloe gin and vodka into a glass of ice. Top off with orange juice.

SPICY WARM NUTS

1 ½ cup pecans

1 ½ cup walnuts

1 ½ cup cashew pieces

1 ½ cup dry roasted peanuts

1 stick melted butter

1 tsp. Cajun seasoning

1 tsp. garlic powder

1 tsp. onion powder

¼ tsp. pepper

¼ tsp. oregano (dried)

¼ tsp. thyme (dried)

3 tsp. Worcestershire sauce

Salt to taste (optional)

Pre heat oven to 325 degrees, combine the first 4 ingredients into a 9x13 dish. Mix all the seasonings together except the salt. Add to melted butter. Stir well. Pour over nuts and roast for 45 minutes. Stir every 20 minutes. Salt to taste.

SPINACH BALLS

Note Freezing required

2 10-ounce boxes of frozen spinach, thoroughly drained

2 c. Italian seasoned bread crumbs

1 ¼ c. shredded Parmesan cheese

1 stick melted butter

2 small green onions, finely chopped

3 eggs

Dash of nutmeg

Mix all ingredients together to form cocktail meatball size about 1 inch balls. Freeze. Place on a cookie sheet and bake at 350 degrees for 13 minutes. Keep and serve warm.

SPINACH BALL SAUCE

½ c. Dijon mustard
½ c. honey
1 egg yolk

Mix honey and mustard, and then add egg yolk. Cook over low heat, stirring constantly, the mixture will thicken slightly. Cover with saran wrap and chill. Serve at room temperature

SPINACH DIP

Overnight refrigeration required

2 pkgs. frozen spinach (chopped)
1 pkg. dry vegetable soup mix
1 8 oz. container sour cream
1 small onion (minced)
1 garlic clove (minced)
½ c. Mayonnaise
1/3 c. finely chopped walnuts (optional)

Thaw spinach, add sour cream, mayonnaise, stir well, and add onion, garlic, vegetable soup mix, and walnuts. Stir well. Refrigerate overnight. Serve with your favorite crackers or bread.

SUB SANDWICH

12 round Kaiser rolls or Hoagie Rolls
1 lb. deli ham lunchmeat

1 lb. hard salami lunchmeat
1 lb. turkey breast lunchmeat
1 lb. sandwich pepperoni
1 lb. sliced mozzarella cheese
1 lb. provolone cheese
1 red onion, thinly sliced
¼ cup Italian Dressing
Italian seasoning

Preheat oven to 350 degrees. Slice Kaiser rolls and lightly brush 1 teaspoon of dressing over each side. Divide the meat among 12 rolls and stack on bottom half of each roll using at least a few slices of salami per roll. Add a few onions on top of the meat, then 2 slices of cheese per roll. Sprinkle lightly with oregano or seasoning and add top of roll. Wrap each in aluminum foil wraps and pop in oven for 15 minutes. Serve warm right out of the foil.

TRAIL MIX

2 cups granola
1 c. coarsely chopped pecans
1 c. coarsely chopped walnuts
1 (3 ½ oz.) can flaked coconut
¾ c. sunflower seeds (meat only)
1 teaspoon ground cinnamon
1 tsp. salt
1 (14-ounce) can sweetened condensed milk
½ c vegetable oil
1 ½ c. banana chips (optional)
1 c. dark raisins
1 c. golden raisins
1 c. dried cherries
1 c. dried apricots, diced

Preheat oven to 300 degrees.

In large mixing bowl, combine all ingredients except banana chips and raisins, cherries and apricots. Mix well with a wooden spoon. Spread evenly in an aluminum foil-lined cookie sheet pan. Bake 55 to 60 minutes, stirring every 15 minutes. Remove from oven; stir in banana chips, raisins, cherries and apricots. Cool thoroughly. Store tightly covered at room temperature.

TROPICAL FRUIT DRINK

2 oz. Pineapple juice
2 oz. Guava juice
2 oz. Papaya juice
2 oz. Mango nectar juice
1 Banana (peeled)
8 strawberries
1 can lemon-lime soda
Ice Cubes
Fresh fruit for garnish

Combine pineapple, juices, banana, strawberries and soda. Pour into a blender over ice cubes and crush until smooth. Garnish with fresh fruit.

Notes

Chapter 2

OOH SOO WET
(Soups & Vegetables)

5 Ingredient Salad

Beef Soup

Candied Yams

Chicken Marinade

Chili

Dirty Rice

Grilled Corn on the Cob

Corn Pudding

Oyster Stew

Potato Salad

Sautéed Greens

Shrimp, Chicken, & Okra Gumbo

Turkey Soup

Vegetarian Chili

Baked Beans

Bourbon Sweet Potatoes

Chicken & Dumplings

Chicken Soup

Creamed Spinach

Fried Wild Rice

Jambalaya

Macaroni and Cheese

Pinto Beans

Potato Soup

Shrimp Creole

Steak and Spinach Salad

Vegetable Stock

5 INGREDIENT SALAD

1 head lettuce chopped
1 tomato chopped
1 medium onion sliced thin
¼ cup mayonnaise
Salt & Pepper to taste

Mix all 4 ingredients together. Add salt & pepper to taste. Serve chilled. Great served with Pinto Beans.

BAKED BEANS

2 cans pork and beans (may use vegetarian beans)
1 tsp. mustard
1 Small onion chopped
¼ c. bar-b-Que sauce (your favorite)
¼ c. ketchup
¼ c. molasses
¼ c. honey
3 Tbsp. brown sugar
3 Tbsp. sugar
3 Strips bacon (cooked and crumbled)(optional)
1 tsp. bacon fat (optional)

In a casserole dish mix all ingredients and bake at 350 degrees for about 45 minutes to 1 hour, covered. (Optional: You may add ground beef or ground turkey to this recipe)

** TIP: You may use turkey or pork bacon, cooked and crumbled. **

BEEF SOUP

1 ½ lb. Beef cubes or stew beef
Salt and Pepper
1 can beef broth
1 Tbsp. Beef flavor bouillon granules
2 Medium onions (diced)
4 carrots (peeled and sliced)
1 medium head of cabbage (chopped)
1 can peas
1 can corn
1 can green beans
1 large can crushed tomatoes
1 Tbsp. Sugar
Mrs. Dash- Spicy

Cook beef cubes and onions with water and add salt and pepper to taste. Cook over medium heat. Add next 10 ingredients. Add the Mrs. Dash season to taste. Reduce heat and cook until carrots are soft.

BOURBON SWEET POTATOES

2 pounds sweet potatoes (peeled and quartered)
4 Tbsp. butter
¼- ½ c. bourbon
3 Tbsp. orange juice
4 Tbsp. light brown sugar
3 Tbsp. white sugar or Splenda
1/4 tsp. cinnamon
1 bag of mini marshmallows (optional)

Boil potatoes until soft (about 30-40 minutes). Drain and add to a large bowl. Add the remaining ingredients. Whip until smooth. Place in a lightly oiled casserole dish. Bake at 350 until lightly browned (about 30-40 minutes). Cover with marshmallows and place back into oven until marshmallows are melted and slightly turning brown.

CANDIED YAMS

6 Sweet Potatoes (peeled and sliced)
1 stick of butter (sliced & cubed))
1/3 c. Brown sugar
1/4 c. White sugar
1 tsp. Vanilla
Cinnamon
Nutmeg
All Spice

Place potatoes in a casserole dish. Sprinkle butter over potatoes. Sprinkle sugars, & vanilla. Top with the next three seasonings. Just Sprinkle a <u>little</u> over the top of potatoes. Do not use a lot of Nutmeg. Cover and bake at 350 degrees for about 1 hour.

TIP: Nutmeg is a strong spice, a little goes a long way

CHICKEN & DUMPLINGS

2 Tbsp. butter
2 Tbsp. Olive oil
1 large yellow onion, chopped
1 clove garlic, minced
1 pound boneless chicken thighs

1 c. low-sodium chicken broth

1 (10 ounce) package frozen mixed vegetables

½ tsp. dried sage

½ tsp. dried thyme

1 ½ cups self-rising flour

3 Tbsp. chopped fresh parsley

3 Tbsp. shortening

2/3 cup buttermilk

Melt butter and olive oil in a large saucepan or pot over medium heat. Sauté onion and garlic for 5 minutes, remove and set to side. Stir in chicken and sauté until browned, about 7 to 10 minutes. Stir in broth, onion and garlic, vegetables, sage and thyme. Mix all together and let simmer over medium low heat while preparing the dumplings. In a medium bowl, mix flour and parsley together. Add shortening and stir mixture into a coarse, dough. Stir in buttermilk, a little bit at a time, until dough holds together and is soft but firm. If needed, add up to 2 tablespoons more buttermilk. Bring chicken mixture to a boil over medium high heat and drop round spoonful of dumpling mixture on top, not touching each other.

Reduce heat to low, cover pot and let simmer for 10 to 12 minutes.

CHICKEN MARINADE

Olive oil

Zesty Italian Dressing

Minced Garlic

Liquid smoke

Mix the four ingredients together in a freezer bag. Put chicken in bag and refrigerate for 1 hour.

CHICKEN SOUP

2 Tbsp. olive oil

2 Tbsp. butter

2 large carrots, peeled and sliced

1 whole chicken, breasts removed and reserved

1 can chicken broth

1 celery stalk, sliced

2 onions, diced

2 Tbsp. minced garlic

½ teaspoon dried thyme

3 quarts boiling water

1/4 cup minced fresh parsley leaves

1 box frozen mixed vegetables

½ bag egg noodles

Salt & pepper

Garlic powder

Poultry seasoning

Chicken flavor bouillon granules

2 bay leaves

Season chicken parts with salt, pepper, garlic powder and poultry seasoning. Set aside. Cut the breast in quarters.

Heat the oil and butter in a large pot and sauté the breasts until they are light brown, about 5 minutes. Remove the breasts and set aside. Add the onions, celery and garlic, salt and pepper onions, celery and garlic, and sauté until translucent, approximately 4 to 5 minutes. Remove and set aside. Cut up the remaining parts of the chicken (not the breasts) into small pieces to allow them to release their juices in the shortest time possible, add the pieces to the pot, and cook for 8 to 10 minutes until no longer pink. Return the breast, onion, celery, garlic to the pot, reduce the heat to low, cover, and simmer until the chicken releases its juices, about 20 minutes. Add boiling water, 1 teaspoons of salt, and bay leaves & chicken bouillon granules. Cover and simmer on low heat for 40 minutes. Add vegetables, thyme and chicken broth; simmer until the vegetables are tender. Pour in egg noodles and cook for 5-8 minutes. Season with salt and pepper, stir well. Add parsley and serve.

CHILI

(Crock pot recipe)

1 ½ lb. ground beef or ground turkey

salt and pepper to taste

2 (15 ounce) cans dark red kidney beans 1 can chili beans

3 (14.5 ounce) cans Mexican-style stewed tomatoes

¼ cup red wine vinegar

4 Tbsp. chili powder

1 tsp. ground cumin

1 tsp. dried parsley

1 ½ Tbsp. white sugar

1 tsp. dried basil

1 dash Worcestershire sauce

½ cup beer (dark ale)
2 Bay leaves

In a large skillet over medium-high heat, cook ground beef until evenly browned. Drain off grease, and season to taste with salt and pepper. In a crock pot, combine the cooked beef or turkey, kidney beans, tomatoes, beer, and red wine vinegar. Season with chili powder, cumin, parsley, sugar, basil and Worcestershire sauce. Stir to distribute ingredients evenly. Add Bay leaves. Cook on High for 6 hours. This recipe can also be cooked on low for 8 hours.

CREAMED SPINACH

3 packages frozen spinach, (10 oz each)
8 oz. cream cheese, softened
1 (8 oz.) package Swiss cheese (chopped)
½ cup butter, melted, divided
1 ½ cups seasoned bread crumbs
1 cup shredded parmesan cheese
2 strips of bacon (cooked and crumbled)
Salt & pepper to taste
paprika

Thaw spinach, put into a cheese cloth, press or squeeze to remove excess water. Grease a casserole dish and set aside. In a large mixing bowl, combine the spinach, cream cheese, Swiss cheese, Parmesan, bacon and ¼ cup of melted butter.

Spoon spinach mixture into casserole dish. Sprinkle with the breadcrumbs and paprika, and drizzle with remaining ¼ cup of butter. Bake at 350 degrees for 25 minutes.

DIRTY RICE

½ c. onion, chopped
½ c. celery leaves, chopped

1 pound fresh Andouille or pork sausage
1 ½ cup white long grain rice, uncooked
3 cups water
2 tsp. ground cumin

In large pot, sauté onion and celery, cook sausage until the sausage is done and crumbled. If sausage produces excess fat, drain. Add rice, water, cumin, onion, celery and browned sausage. Stir ingredients together and bring to a boil. Cover, reduce heat to low, and simmer for 20 minutes or until rice is tender.

> **Tip: When cooking rice use a ratio of 2 to 1. 2 cups water to 1 cup rice.

FRIED WILD RICE

2 cups Wild rice (cooked)
4 strips Bacon (cooked and crumbled)
½ tsp. garlic minced
2 Tbsp. onion diced
1 Tbsp. celery diced
1 carrot (peeled and diced)
¼ cup oyster sauce
1 Egg (lightly beaten)

In a large skillet or wok cook the bacon, add the onion, celery and carrot. Cook mixture until the carrots are soft. Add the garlic, stir well. Next, add the cooked rice and cook for a couple of minutes longer. Add the oyster sauce and fold gently. Slowly whisk in the egg and cook for about 2 minutes.

GRILLED CORN ON THE COB

6 fresh ears of corn

4 Tbsp. butter

3 Tbsp. horseradish sauce

2 Tbsp. Dijon mustard

1 teaspoon snipped fresh thyme (or 1/4 tsp. if dried, crushed)

1 tsp. dried parsley

¼ tsp. crushed red pepper flakes

salt and pepper to taste (after cooked) (optional)

Peel husk and remove the silk from corn. (you can use a stiff brush or your fingers, to remove silk from corn). Place each cob individually in heavy duty aluminum foil. In a sauce pan add the next 3 ingredients until butter melts and stir occasionally use a spatula or a wooden spoon. Add the next 2 ingredients and stir. Brush the mixture on to the corn and wrap tightly. Place on an uncovered grill over medium hot coals and grill for 25-30 minutes. Don't forget to turn corn every 10 minutes.

**TIP WHEN PICKING FRESH CORN:
Corn converts from sugar to starch as it ages. The varieties

of corn, Super Sweet and Summer Sweet, retain their sugar much longer. Be sure to select corn with full ears (mature), fresh green husks and silks free from break-down or decay. Peel back the husk and observe the kernels which should be even, full and plump.

JAMBALAYA

½ c. oil
2 Tbsp. garlic (minced)
1 c. onion (chopped)
1 ½ c. cooked ham cubes
1 c. chicken chopped or cubed (cooked)
1 lb. raw shrimp, peeled and deveined
1 lb. Kielbasa sausage (sliced)
½ c. finely chopped green onions
3 Tbsp. finely chopped bell pepper
2 cloves garlic minced
2 (8-oz.) can tomato sauce
2 tsp. Worcestershire sauce
¼ tsp. cayenne pepper
3 c. chicken stock
4-½ Tbsp. Creole seasoning
1 bay leaf
2 Tbsp. fresh parsley (minced)
Salt and Pepper to taste
3/4-cup rice (may be cooked and served separately in a small sauce pan)

In a large skillet cook your ham, chicken, sausage, onion, green pepper, garlic, until onions are transparent about 7 minutes. Put all ingredients except shrimp into a large pot and bring to a boil. Lower the heat to a low heat and let simmer for 30 minutes. Add shrimp and stir well. Cook for additional 10 minutes. If you did not put rice in this dish serve over rice that you cooked separately.

CORN PUDDING

2 1/2 cups drained corn
3 to 4 eggs well beaten
1 cup unsifted all-purpose flour
1 to 1 1/4 cup sugar
2 cans of evaporated milk
Nutmeg
2 tbs. melted butter

Heat oven 325 degrees, lightly grease casserole dish. In large bowl combine drained corn and eggs, mix well combine flour, and mix well. Add sugar, mix well. Combine melted butter and 2 dashes of nutmeg. Add evaporated milk; pour into a very lightly greased casserole dish. Place casserole dish in a larger dish containing 1 inch of hot water. Bake uncovered 1 hr. and 10 minutes. Stick knife in middle, when it comes out clean it's done.

MACARONI & CHEESE

6 oz. elbow macaroni noodles

1 tsp. dry mustard

2 cups shredded cheddar cheese

2 cups Monterey Jack & Colby cheese

3 oz. Velveeta cheese cut into cubes

2 oz. sour cream

2 large cans Evaporated milk

1 stick butter

3 eggs (beaten)

Salt and Pepper to taste

1 c. sharp shredded cheddar cheese (for topping)

Boil macaroni noodles until done. Drain off water, put back into the pot you used to cook noodles in. Spray casserole dish with a non-stick spray. Put butter in noodles and let melt. Season the noodles with salt and pepper and dry mustard, and sour cream. Stir well to coat the noodles using a wooden spoon. Place 2 c. shredded cheese, 2 cups jack and Colby cheese, Velveeta, 1 can evaporated milk into a sauce pan and stir until cheese is melted. This will make a sauce for your Mac and cheese. Pour in the sauce mix. Stir well. Mix eggs and another can of evaporated milk together, add salt and pepper, pour over noodle mixture stirring very well. Texture should be the same texture as cake batter. Pour mixture into the greased casserole dish. Top with sharp cheddar cheese. Cover and bake at 350 degrees until done.

(Mixture is solid)

OYSTER STEW

4 cups whole milk

4 cups half and half

2/3 stick of butter

7 cups of fresh oysters, un-drained

½ c. finely chopped onion

2 Tbsp. fresh parsley chopped

2 Tbsp. Pimento chopped

2 tsp. salt

1 tsp. pepper

1 Tsp. Worcestershire sauce

In Dutch oven pan, combine milk and cream together. Heat slowly. DO NOT BOIL.

In a medium pan, melt butter. Add onion and oysters, cook for 10 minutes over low heat. Stir in parsley, pimento, salt, pepper and Worcestershire sauce into hot milk. Stir frequently on low heat. **DO NOT BOIL**. Serve with Oyster crackers.

PINTO BEANS

1 small bag of Pinto beans (soaked in warm water for ½ hour)

1 large ham hock or (you can use a large piece of smoked turkey)

1 medium onion chopped

2 cloves garlic (minced)

1 red bell pepper chopped finely

1 Tbsp. salt

½ Tbsp. pepper

1½ tsp. sugar

1 tsp. ground Cumin

1 ½ tsp. Chili powder

½ tsp. crushed red pepper

Drain and rinse beans. Place into a Dutch oven pot ham hocks and water. Bring hock to a boil. Add beans, spices, onions, garlic and red pepper to water and stir. Cover and place on a low to medium - low heat. Cook until beans are tender. Water will form a thick gravy when beans are done. Stir occasionally. You may need to add more water during the cooking process. Add 1 cup at a time.

POTATO SALAD

6 potatoes large Red potatoes

3 eggs

Water

½ small onion (finely chopped)

1 stalk celery (finely chopped)

¼ c. sweet relish

1 tsp. sugar

¼ c. mayonnaise

1 Tbsp. mustard

Salt & pepper to taste

Put potatoes & eggs in a large Dutch oven pot, with cold water 2 inches above the potatoes. Cover & bring to a boil. Cook until potatoes and are tender; drain and cool. Peel potatoes and slice 1/4-inch thick; Chop eggs and set aside. Using your hands mix in celery, onion, salt, pepper, sugar and relish. Add mayonnaise and mustard. Depending on how you like your potato salad you may need to add a little more mayonnaise.

> **Tip: add mayonnaise if you need more 1 Tbsp. at a time.)
> Mix well. Refrigerate.

POTATO SOUP

1 pound bacon, cooked & chopped
2 stalks celery, diced
1 onion, chopped
3 cloves garlic, minced
8 potatoes, peeled and cubed
4 ½ cups chicken stock,
3 tablespoons butter
1/4 cup all-purpose flour
1 cup heavy cream
1 teaspoon dried tarragon
3 teaspoons chopped fresh cilantro
salt and pepper to taste

In a Dutch oven, cook the bacon over medium heat until done. Remove bacon from pan, and set aside. Drain off all but 1/4 cup of the bacon grease. In the bacon grease remaining in the pan, sauté the celery and onion until onion begins to turn clear. Add the garlic, and continue cooking for 1 to 2 minutes. Add the cubed potatoes, and toss to coat. Sauté for 3 to 4 minutes. Return the bacon to the pan, and add enough chicken stock to just cover the potatoes. Cover, and simmer until potatoes are tender. In a separate pan, melt the butter over medium heat. Whisk in the flour. Cook stirring constantly, for 1 to 2 minutes. Whisk in the heavy cream, tarragon and cilantro. Bring the cream mixture to a boil, and cook, stirring constantly, until thickened. Stir the cream mixture into the potato mixture. Puree about 1/2 the soup, and return to the pan. Adjust seasonings to taste.

SAUTEED GREENS

2 bunches of greens (Collard, Kale, Mustard, Turnip, Spinach, Tender or Rape, (washed & chopped)
½ medium Onion (chopped)
3 Tbsp. Olive Oil (Extra Virgin)
4 Tbsp. Butter (unsalted)
Crushed red pepper flakes
1 cap full of cider vinegar
Pinch of sugar about 1 tsp. (optional)
Garlic powder
1 clove minced garlic
Salt & Pepper (to taste)
¼ to ½ cup of Vegetable broth or stock

In a large pot, heat olive oil and butter until butter is melted. Add onion, minced garlic. Sauté until the onion and garlic becomes soft. Add greens, red pepper flakes, garlic powder, salt & pepper and sugar. Stir well. Lower heat, Cover and simmer until desired doneness. You may need to add more salt, pepper & garlic powder during the cooking process. (I usually cook mine for about 45 minutes on low heat. Make sure you check your liquid level and **do not** let the liquid boil out. Add broth when the level gets low if needed to cook longer.

> **TIP: The liquid from the greens is known as POT LIQ-UOR!!!! For better flavored greens add about 1 lb. of tender greens or spinach to the collard greens. You can mix the greens or just use one kind. If you use spinach add in about 15 minutes before dish is finished. It does not take spinach long to cook.

Kale

Collard Greens

SHRIMP CREOLE

2 tablespoons canola oil or extra virgin olive oil

1/2 c. onion (chopped)

1/2 c. green bell pepper (chopped)

1/4 c. celery (chopped)

2 cloves garlic (minced)

1 teaspoon Creole seasoning

1/4 teaspoon cayenne pepper to taste

1 14.5 ounce can of diced tomatoes (un-drained)

1/4 c. white wine, water,

1 can tomato sauce

1 Bay Leaf

1 pound fresh, raw Shrimp (cleaned, shelled, and deveined)

sliced green onion and chopped fresh parsley

Heat oil over medium heat and sauté vegetables until tender, about 4-5 minutes. Add cloves. Cook one minute more. Sprinkle vegetables with Creole seasoning and cayenne pepper. Stir mixture thoroughly. Add diced tomatoes and white wine, water, tomato juice, or tomato sauce. Add bay leaf. Bring mixture to a boil. Cover, reduce heat to low and simmer 10 minutes. Add shrimp. Simmer, covered, 4-5 minutes or until shrimp is opaque. Remove bay leaf and discard. Check seasoning and add salt and pepper and additional spice to taste. (Some Louisiana cooks swear by adding a pinch of sugar and a dash of hot sauce at the end of the dish.) Do not forget to remove the bay leaf.

SHRIMP, CHICKEN AND OKRA GUMBO

1 Roll of Beef Sausage (sliced) or Kielbasa

2 Tbsp. olive oil

1 large onion (chopped)

4 stalks of celery (chopped)

1 large green pepper (chopped)

4 cloves garlic (chopped)

5 scallions (chopped)

1 lb. Okra chopped

1 lb. cooked chicken pulled off bone and cut up in chunks

2 lbs. Shrimp (shelled & deveined)

4 ½ c. Shrimp stock (use shells to make stock)

1 bottle DARK beer

5 large blanched tomatoes with skin removed (chopped)

1 tsp. black pepper

1/2 tsp. Cayenne pepper

1Tbsp. Cajun seasoning

1 1/2 tsp. Salt

1 tsp. Thyme

Sauté sausage. Remove. In a pot add next 6 ingredients stirring well until onions are almost translucent. Add tomatoes, okra, sausage, chicken, beer, broth, and seasonings cover and let reduce. Add shrimp and cook until shrimp turns pink stirring occasionally.

Tip: Shrimp stock, boil shrimp shells for about 20 minutes.

STEAK AND SPINACH SALAD

6 cups fresh spinach, rinsed and dried

½ c. dried cranberries

½ c. walnut halves

1 tomato, sliced

1 pound top round steak, thinly sliced

1 pinch salt

1 pinch ground black pepper

Arrange spinach on a large plate. Sprinkle with cranberries and walnuts, and arrange tomato slices on top. Set aside. In a non-stick skillet (or a regular skillet coated with non-stick spray) cook steak over medium heat until no pink remains and steak is thoroughly cooked. Arrange cooked steak over salad. Sprinkle salt and pepper on top, and drizzle with your favorite dressing.

> **Tip: Season steak before cooking. Let it rest in the refrigerator for at least 1 hour**

TURKEY SOUP

1 picked over turkey
3 large carrots, chopped
1 (15 ounce) can cut green beans, drained
1 cup chopped celery
1 cup chopped cabbage(small pieces)
1 bag of baby carrots
½ cup chopped onion
2 cups white rice
3 cups water
3 cups of Vegetable stock

Pick your turkey nearly clean. We are not real concerned about the choice of meat here. Put the turkey, including the juices, into vegetable stock in a large pot. Add green beans, celery, cabbage, baby carrots and onions. Simmer on low for 1 hour. Cook white rice and set aside. Add rice and continue to simmer on low for 30 more minutes.

> **Tip: instead of using 6 cups of water, use 3 cups water and 3 cups vegetable stock., For leftover Turkey: turkey salad is great for a few days, or even turkey potpie**

VEGETABLE STOCK

2 medium Onions (chopped)
3 medium Carrots (chopped)
3 ribs Celery (chopped)
1 cup Parsley w/stems
3 cloves Garlic, crushed
½ tsp. Thyme
2 Bay leaves
2 quarts Water
To taste Salt and pepper

Place all ingredients in a large soup pot. Bring to a boil, reduce the heat and simmer uncovered for 45 minutes. Strain and use immediately or refrigerate (or freeze) until needed.

VEGETARIAN CHILI

1 Tbsp. olive oil
1 onion, chopped
2 red bell pepper, seeded and chopped
1 jalapeno pepper, seeded and minced
10 fresh mushrooms, quartered
6 Roma (plum) tomatoes, diced
1 cup fresh corn kernels
1 tsp. ground black pepper
1 tsp. ground cumin
2 ½ Tbsp. chili powder
2 (15 ounce) cans black beans, drained and rinsed
2 cups chicken broth
1 tsp. salt

Heat oil in a large saucepan, over medium-high heat. Sautee the onion, red bell peppers, jalapeno, mushrooms, tomatoes and corn for 10 minutes or until the onions are translucent. Season with black pepper, cumin and chili powder. Stir in the black beans, chicken broth and salt. bring to a boil. Remove 1 1/2 cups of the soup put in food processor or blender; puree and stir the bean mixture back into the soup.

Notes

Chapter 3

BEAT YOU WITH A WET NOODLE
(Pasta & Casseroles)

Angel Hair with Crab Sauce

Bean & Meat Casserole

Breakfast Casserole

Breakfast Casserole with a Twist

Cheese Manicotti

Creamy Chicken & Noodle Casserole

Ham & Cheese Quiche

Manicotti

Peachy's Hamburger Casserole

Shrimp and Grits

Spicy Pasta

Sweet Potato & Apple Casserole

Baked Ziti

Bow Tie & Seafood Casserole

Breakfast Casserole 2

Broccoli Casserole

Chicken Enchilada Casserole

Ground Turkey Casserole

Lasagna

Parmesan Linguine

Seafood Enchilada

Spicy Bean Casserole

Spinach Lasagna

NOTE: Pasta dishes made in this chapter, I like to use a multigrain or whole wheat pasta whenever possible.

ANGEL HAIR WITH CRAB SAUCE

1/3 cup olive oil
½ cup chopped onion
3 cloves garlic, minced
¾ c chicken broth
1 ½ tsp. basil leaves
1 tsp. seafood seasoning
½ tsp. marjoram leaves
½ tsp. salt
¼ tsp. freshly ground pepper
1 (28 oz.) can whole plum tomatoes, chopped
1 (12 oz.) package angel hair Pasta, uncooked
2 (6 oz.) cans lump crabmeat, drained

Heat oil in large skillet, over medium heat, add onion, and cook until soft about 2 minutes. Add garlic, cook 1 minute. Add wine and seasonings. Heat to boiling, cook 1 minute.
Add tomatoes with juice, return to boiling. Cook 5 minutes stirring occasionally. Meanwhile, cook pasta according to package directions. Toss hot pasta with sauce and crabmeat and serve immediately.

BAKED ZITI
(Jordan's Favorite)

1 (16 ounce) package rigatoni pasta
1 lb. lean ground beef (optional)
1 onion, chopped
2 (28 ounce) jars spaghetti sauce
6 oz. sliced provolone cheese
6 oz. sliced mozzarella cheese

8 oz. ricotta cheese

1 c. sour cream

½ c. grated Parmesan cheese

¼ c. chopped fresh basil

Bring a large pot of lightly salted water to a boil. Add pasta and cook for 8 to 10 minutes or until al dente; drain. In a large skillet, brown beef over medium heat and add onions; sauté until no longer pink. Drain off fat and add spaghetti sauce; simmer for about 15 minutes. Add ricotta cheese and sour cream mix well. Preheat oven to 350 degrees. In a lightly greased 2-quart baking dish, place about half of the pasta; top with a layer of provolone and mozzarella cheese slices. Spread on a layer of half the spaghetti sauce mixture. Cover with remaining pasta, cheese and sauce; sprinkle a layer of Parmesan cheese and fresh basil. Bake in preheated oven for about 30 minutes or until cheese and sauce are bubbly.

BEAN & MEAT CASSEROLE

1 tsp. garlic (minced)

1 medium onion (chopped)

2 c. cooked cubed ham

2 lb. pork sausage (cooked)

2 tsp. dried parsley

1 can navy beans or great white northern beans (drained)

1/3 c. white wine

1 can tomato sauce

¼ tsp. ground cloves

1 tsp. dried thyme

½ tsp. sugar

Salt and pepper to taste

Preheat oven to 325 degrees. Sauté garlic, and onion in a skillet. Add the next 10 ingredients and mix well. Pour into a 9x13 casserole dish. Cover and bake for 45 minutes.

BOW TIE & SEAFOOD CASSEROLE

2 eggs (beaten)
1 c. ½ & ½
1 c. Heavy whipping cream
1 c. Swiss cheese
½ c. feta cheese (tomato & basil)
½ tsp. Basil (dried)
1/8 tsp. Red pepper flakes
¼ tsp. salt
¼ tsp. pepper
8 oz. bow tie pasta (cooked)
1 jar salsa
1 lb. Shrimp (peeled & deveined)
1 lb. Scallops
2 c. Monterey Jack cheese

Spray a 9x13 baking dish. Mix together the first 9 ingredients together in a bowl. Place a layer of pasta in baking dish. Put a layer of salsa, next place a layer of shrimp and scallops. Sprinkle 1 cup of Monterey Jack cheese. Repeat layering process ending with cheese. Bake at 350 for 35 minutes.

BREAKFAST CASSEROLE

4 slices bread
1 roll Sausage (Hot)
1 roll Sausage (Regular)
1 small onion chopped
1 medium green pepper chopped
2 c. Shredded cheddar cheese
2 c. milk
8 eggs

Salt and pepper

1 can mushrooms (optional)

Brown sausage; drain grease. Place bread in casserole dish (9x13). Sprinkle sausage over bread. Sprinkle 2 c. cheese. Mix egg and milk together, add green peppers and onion. Stir well. Pour over sausage mixture. Cover and bake at 350 degrees until eggs are hard and firm. Start checking after 50 minutes of baking. (I used Jimmy Dean sausage)

BREAKFAST CASSEROLE 2

6 eggs

1 c. milk

6 oz. cheddar cheese, grated

1-lb sausage or bacon, crumbled

4 Hash brown patties, frozen

1 tsp. salt

1/2 tsp. pepper

1/2 tsp. dry mustard

1/2 c. chopped onion

Line an 8x8 baking dish with frozen hash browns. Sprinkle hash browns with crumbled sausage or bacon. Mix together eggs, milk, salt, pepper, and dry mustard. Pour over meat and hash browns. Top with grated cheddar cheese. Refrigerate overnight. Bake in a preheated oven at 350 degrees for 45 minutes to 1 hour.

BREAKFAST CASSEROLE WITH A TWIST

3/4 lb. ground pork sausage

1 Tbsp. butter

4 green onions, chopped

1/2 lb. fresh mushrooms, sliced

10 eggs, beaten

1 (16 oz.) container low-fat cottage cheese

1 lb. Monterey Jack cheese, shredded

2 (4 oz.) cans diced green Chile peppers, drained

1 c. all-purpose flour

1 tsp. baking powder

1/2 tsp. salt

1/3 c. butter, melted

Place sausage in a large, deep skillet. Cook over medium-high heat until evenly brown. Drain, and set aside. Melt butter in skillet, and cook and stir the green onions and mushrooms until tender. In a large bowl, mix the eggs, cottage cheese, Monterey Jack cheese, and chilies. Stir in the sausage, green onions, and mushrooms. Cover, and refrigerate overnight. Preheat oven to 350 degrees. Lightly grease a 9x13 inch baking dish. In a bowl, sift together the flour, baking powder, and salt. Blend in the melted butter. Stir the flour mixture into the egg mixture. Pour into the prepared baking dish.

BROCCOLI CASSEROLE

2 packages frozen chopped broccoli

1 can cream of chicken soup

1/2 cup mayonnaise

1/2 package Pepperidge farm dressing

3/4 stick butter

Cook broccoli 10 to 12 minutes; drain. Add remaining ingredients. Mix well. Pour into a lightly greased baking dish. Bake at 350 degrees for 30 minutes.

> ** TIP: You can add shredded cheese on top after you take it
> out of the oven. Lightly cover to let cheese melt) **

CHEESE MANICOTTI

1 large onion; minced
1 lb. mushrooms, sliced
1/2 c. butter or margarine
1/2 c. flour
4 cups milk
1 1/2 cups parmesan cheese, grated
Salt and pepper to taste
12 manicotti shells
1 lb. deli-style ricotta
4 oz. mozzarella cheese, diced
1/2 c. Romano cheese, grated
1/4 c. parsley, chopped
3 eggs
1 dash nutmeg

Sauté onion and mushrooms in butter 5 minutes; stir in flour. Gradually stir in milk; stir over low heat until sauce bubbles and thickens. Stir in 1 cup Parmesan cheese and salt and pepper to taste; set aside. Cook manicotti shells according to package directions; drain and cover with cold water. Mix together ricotta, mozzarella, Romano and the remaining Parmesan cheese; add parsley and eggs. Season to taste with salt, and pepper. Add a dash of nutmeg. Drain manicotti shells; stuff with cheese mixture. Place shells side by side in a greased shallow baking pan; spoon sauce over all. Bake in preheated 400 degree oven 20 to 25 minutes, or until bubbly and golden.

CHICKEN ENCHILADA CASSEROLE

6 chicken quarters (boiled and skinned)
1 can chicken broth
1 can chili (with or without beans)
1 can cream of chicken soup

1 can green chilies

1 tsp. jalapeno peppers (finely chopped) (optional)

1 bag of tortilla chips

1 package of your favorite brand of Taco seasoning

4 cups Mexican shredded cheese

Chop cooked chicken and set aside. In a large skillet or large pot, add the next 5 ingredients and mix well. Add Taco seasoning to chicken and coat evenly. Fold in chicken and mix well. In a casserole dish, layer a layer of tortilla chips. Add a layer of chicken mixture. Place a thin layer of cheese. Repeat layers of chips, chicken mixture and finish with a medium to thick layer of cheese. Cover and bake at 350 until cheese is melted.

CREAMY CHICKEN & NOODLE CASSEROLE

1 lb. skinless boneless chicken breast halves

1½ c. water

2 large garlic cloves, minced

1 bay leaf

1/3 c. all-purpose flour

2 Tbsp. cornstarch

2 cups low-fat milk

1 tsp. dried tarragon

1 tsp. salt

1/8 tsp. ground nutmeg

¼ c dry white wine

1 10-ounce package frozen spinach, thawed and squeezed dry

8 oz. spinach fettuccine or fettuccine

8 oz. mushrooms, sliced

1 ½ tsp. olive oil

¾ cup coarse breadcrumbs

¼ cup freshly grated Parmesan cheese

Combine chicken, 1 cup water, garlic and bay leaf in large saucepan. Cover and simmer just until chicken is cooked through, turning once, about 15 minutes. Transfer chicken to plate; cool. Shred chicken. Pour cooking liquid into measuring cup, adding more water to measure 1 cup if necessary. Save cooking liquid. Whisk flour and cornstarch in heavy large saucepan. Add 1 cup milk; whisk until smooth. Stir in 1 cup milk, tarragon, salt, nutmeg and reserved 1 cup chicken cooking liquid. Stir over medium heat until mixture thickens and boils, about 5 minutes. Add wine; stir until mixture is very thick, about 2 minutes longer. Remove from heat. Stir in shredded chicken and spinach. (This can be made 1 day ahead. Cover and chill. Reheat over medium-low heat, stirring frequently, before continuing.) Preheat oven to 400 degrees. Oil a 9x13 glass baking dish. Cook fettuccine in large pot of boiling salted water until just tender but still firm (Al dente) Drain. Return to pot. Add mushrooms and chicken mixture; toss. Season the casserole with salt and pepper. Transfer to a prepared baking dish. Heat oil in small nonstick skillet over medium-high heat. Add breadcrumbs; stir 1 minute. Sprinkle over casserole. Bake until casserole bubbles and breadcrumbs are golden, about 20 minutes. Let stand 10 minutes. Sprinkle with Parmesan.

GROUND TURKEY CASSEROLE

1 lb. ground turkey
1 (15 ounce) can tomato sauce
1 tsp. white sugar
1 (8 ounce) container sour cream
1 (8 ounce) package cream cheese
1 (12 ounce) package uncooked egg noodles
2 cups shredded Cheddar cheese

Preheat oven to 350 degrees . In a large skillet over medium-high heat, sauté the ground turkey for 5 to 10 minutes, or until browned. Drain the turkey, stir in the tomato sauce and sugar, and set aside. In a medium bowl, combine the sour cream and cream cheese. Mix well and set aside. Cook noodles according to package directions. Place them into a 9x13-inch baking dish; layer the turkey mixture over the noodles. Then layer the sour cream mixture over the turkey, and top with cheese. Bake at 350 degrees for 20 to 35 minutes.

HAM AND CHEESE QUICHE

2 tablespoons all-purpose flour
1/2 teaspoon salt
1 cup half-and-half
3 eggs
2 slices Swiss cheese
1 9 inch single crust pie
1/2 cup chopped fresh spinach
1/2 cup canned mushrooms
1 (4.5 ounce) can ham, flaked
1/2 cup shredded Cheddar cheese

Preheat oven to 350 degrees. Beat together flour, salt, half-and-half and eggs in a medium bowl. Place Swiss cheese flat in the pie crust. Arrange spinach evenly over Swiss cheese, then cover with mushrooms. Pour the flour and egg mixture over mushrooms. Cover with flaked ham and top with Cheddar cheese. Bake in the preheated oven 45 to 55 minutes, until surface is golden brown and center is solid.

> **TIP: You can substitute ham and cheese with Lump crab and shrimp with Monterey Jack and Swiss cheese for a sea-food Quiche. Broccoli and Chicken with Colby and Cheddar cheese for a chicken and broccoli quiche. Leak, Spinach and Swiss cheese for a spinach quiche **

LASAGNA

6 Lasagna noodles
1 ½ lb. ground beef
1 ½ lb. ground turkey
1 Tbsp. butter
1 medium onion (chopped)
2 cloves garlic (minced)
1 green pepper (chopped)
8 oz. Ricotta cheese
2 c. Mozzarella cheese (shredded)
3 c. Cheddar cheese (shredded)
Parmesan cheese
Season Salt
Mrs. Dash (original)
1 Tbsp. Italian seasoning
1 ½ jar of your favorite spaghetti sauce

In a large pot boil lasagna noodles until they are al dente. In a skillet, melt butter and add onion and garlic, and green pepper. Cook until soft. Remove, and put into a small bowl. Crumble your ground beef and turkey in a skillet. Season with season salt, and Mrs. Dash . Cook until done. Drain the water off of your lasagna noodles and place a layer into a 9 x13 casserole dish. Drain the liquid off of the meat. Add the onion mixture, Italian seasoning, and the ricotta cheese to the meat mixture in the large pot. Pour your favorite spaghetti sauce and mix well. Spoon the first layer of meat mixture on top of your noodles. Sprinkle with parmesan cheese. Top with mozzarella and cheddar cheese. Layer with noodles and repeat the steps again.

> **Tip: You may use all ground beef or all ground turkey. Use 3lbs. Instead of 1 ½ of each.

Your final topping should be mozzarella and cheddar cheese. Spray aluminum foil lightly with a cooking spray. Cover dish and bake at 350 degrees for 40 minutes. Let stand for 10 minutes.

MANICOTTI (meat)

SAUCE
1/4 c. olive oil
1 ½ lb. ground beef or turkey (cooked)
½ c. minced onion
1 minced garlic clove
1-32 oz. can tomatoes cut up
1-6 oz can tomato paste
2 tsp. salt
2 tsp. brown sugar
1 tsp. oregano
1 tsp. basil leaves
1 tsp. parsley
¼ tsp. pepper

FILLING
1 lb. ground beef or turkey
4 Tbsp. minced green onion
1 tsp. salt
¼ tsp. pepper
1 lb. ricotta cheese
2 cups grated mozzarella
1 egg beaten
1 tsp. parsley
1-8oz. box manicotti

Cook drain and cool ground beef or turkey. In a separate bowl mix filling. Combine sauce with beef, stuff manicotti shells with filling. Divide sauce, spread sauce on pan bottom. Place stuffed manicotti shells on top of the sauce. Cover manicotti shells with remaining sauce, sprinkle with Parmesan cheese. Bake covered for 30-40 min. at a 350 degree oven.

PARMESAN LINGUINE

½ pound Linguine (dry)
4 Tablespoons Butter
¾ c. Parmesan, grated
To taste Salt and pepper

Cook the pasta in boiling water until done. Drain, but do not rinse. Return to the pot. Toss in the remaining ingredients and warm over low heat until the butter and cheese melts (about 1 minute). Serve immediately as a side dish.

PEACHY'S HAMBURGER CASSEROLE

1 - 1 1/2 lb. ground beef (browned and drained) or ground turkey.
1 small can green peas (drained)
1 cup cooked curly noodles (pasta)
1 jar spaghetti sauce (I use Prego Mushrooms)
1 tsp. sugar in spaghetti sauce
2 cups cheddar cheese (shredded)
1 onion chopped (sauté)

Brown ground beef, or turkey, drain grease. Add pasta twist and stir. Add onion stir. Add peas, stir. Add spaghetti sauce, 1 cup cheese, stir well. Put into a casserole dish that has been sprayed with a vegetable oil. Put remaining cheese on top and bake at 350 degrees for 20 minutes, or until cheese is melted.

SEAFOOD ENCHILADA

12 (12 inch) flour tortillas
8 ounces Monterey Jack cheese, shredded
1 (6 oz.) can crab meat, drained
1 pound cooked medium shrimp, shelled and deveined
1 (20 oz.) can enchilada sauce
1 (8 oz.) container sour cream

Preheat oven to 350 degrees. Lay tortillas on a flat surface. In the middle of each tortilla place equal amounts of cheese, crab, and shrimp. Set aside some cheese to sprinkle on top of the tortillas. Roll the tortillas to form enchiladas. Arrange side by side in a 9x13 inch baking pan. Pour green enchilada sauce over all of the enchiladas; the green sauce should cover the enchiladas completely. Sprinkle the remaining cheese over the enchiladas. Cover, and bake for 30 minutes in the preheated oven. Remove cover, and continue baking 15 minutes. Top enchiladas with sour cream and green onions and serve.

SHRIMP AND GRITS

Grits
1 Tbsp. Butter
¼ tsp. Garlic Powder
Crushed Red Pepper
Dash Salt
1 cup sharp Cheddar Cheese
1 lb. Jumbo Shrimp (peeled and deveined)
¼ cup White wine or Champagne
Old Bay seafood seasoning
1 tsp. minced Garlic
Garlic powder
Chopped Parsley
1 Tbsp. + 1 tsp. Olive oil

In a freezer or storage bag, add shrimp, wine, Old Bay, garlic, garlic powder, 2 shakes crushed red pepper and parsley. Stir well. Let stand for at least 20 minutes. Best if marinated overnight.

Cook Grits by direction on box. Add butter, garlic powder, 1 shake of crushed red pepper and salt. Stir well. Cover and cook until grits are almost done. Add cheddar cheese, turn heat to low and cover. Make sure you keep stirring so it does not stick.

Heat Olive oil in a skillet, pour shrimp and mixture into the skillet and sauté until shrimp is done. Spoon grits into a bowl and then cover with shrimp and juice.

(Optional: You may add red, yellow and orange peppers to this dish. Sauté them first before adding shrimp)

SPICY BEAN CASSEROLE

1 Tbsp. butter
1 medium onion (finely chopped)
1 green pepper (finely chopped)
½ red pepper (finely chopped)
2 Tbsp. garlic (minced)

3 ½ c. water

1 can black bean (drained)

1 can pinto bean (drained)

1 can corn

1 can tomato sauce

1 ½ packages of taco seasoning mix

1 box jiffy corn muffin mix

Melt butter in a skillet, sauté onion, peppers, and garlic until vegetables are soft. Add water, corn, beans, tomato sauce, and seasonings. Simmer for 25 minutes. Grease a casserole dish. Follow instructions on corn muffin mix. Put bean mixture in casserole dish and top with corn muffin mix. Bake uncovered for 20 minutes at a 400 degree oven.

SPICY PASTA

3 Tbsp. Olive oil

1 lb. Chicken (boneless breast (diced)

½ lb. Andouille sausage (sliced)

½ c. Peppers (diced)

½ c. Onions (diced)

1 tsp. Garlic (minced)

3 tsp. Cajun seasonings

½ c. Tomatoes (diced)

2 cups Chicken broth

5 cups Fettuccine (cooked)

Heat the oil in a large skillet. Cook the peppers and onions and cook until soft. Remove, and place in a small bowl. Cook chicken until tender. Add the peppers and onion mixture. Toss in the sausage, garlic and tomatoes. Cook for 1 minute. Add the seasoning and broth. Cook for 3 minutes. Toss in the cooked pasta and heat. Serve warm.

SPINACH LASAGNA

8 lasagna noodles

2 tablespoons olive oil

2 c. chopped fresh mushrooms

1 chopped onion

1 Tbsp. minced garlic

8 cups fresh spinach

2 cups ricotta cheese

2/3 c. grated Romano cheese

2 tsp. salt

2 tsp. dried oregano

2 tsp. dried basil leaves

1 tsp. ground black pepper

2 egg

4 cups mozzarella cheese (shredded)

1 jar spaghetti sauce (divided)

Preheat oven to 350 degrees . Bring a large pot of lightly salted water to a boil. Add lasagna noodles and cook for 8 to 10 minutes or until al dente; drain. In a skillet over medium-high heat, cook mushrooms, onions, and garlic in olive oil until onions are tender. Drain excess liquid and cool. Boil spinach for 5 minutes. Drain, squeeze out excess liquid. Chop spinach. Combine ricotta, Romano, spinach, salt, oregano, basil, pepper, and eggs in a bowl. Add cooled mushroom mixture. Lay 4 lasagna noodles in bottom of a 9X13 inch baking dish. Spread 2 cups of the cheese/spinach mixture over noodles. Sprinkle 1 cup mozzarella and 1/3 cup parmesan on top. Spread 1/2 jar spaghetti sauce over cheese. Repeat layering. Cover dish with aluminum foil and bake for 1 hour. Cool 20 minutes before serving.

SWEET POTATO & APPLE CASSEROLE

1 large (1/4 lb.) sweet potato

3 medium Golden Delicious apples

1 tsp. lemon juice

1/4 c (1/2 stick) butter or margarine, softened

1/4 tsp. Salt

1/8 tsp. ground pepper

1/4 cups apple juice

2 Tbsp. unseasoned bread crumbs

1 Tbsp. brown sugar

Preheat oven to 350. Peel and thinly slice sweet potato. Peel, core, and cut apples into 1/4-inch-thick slices. Place apples in bowl and add water to cover; add lemon juice. Drain apples well; pat dry. Grease 1 1/2-quart casserole with 1 tablespoon butter. Place one third of apples in bottom of casserole; top with one third of sweet potato. Season with salt and pepper. Repeat to make 2 more layers. Dot top of casserole with 2 tablespoons butter; pour apple juice over all. Cover tightly with lid or aluminum foil and bake 45 minutes. To make topping, in small saucepan, melt remaining 1 tablespoon butter; stir in bread crumbs and brown sugar until well combined. Uncover casserole and sprinkle with topping. Bake uncovered 10 to 15 minutes longer or until potato slices are tender.

Notes

Chapter 4

BUN IN THE OVEN
(Breads)

Banana Muffins

Blueberry Muffins

Bread Pudding

Breakfast Bread

Corn Bread

Grand Ma Rosa's 60 Minute Rolls

Grand Ma Rosa's Dinner Rolls

Grand Ma Rosa's Spoon Bread

Johnny Cakes

Pumpkin Spice Bread

Pumpkin Spice Muffins

Sweet Potato Bread

Sweet Potato Pudding

Whiskey Sauce

BANANA MUFFINS

1 ½ cups all-purpose flour
1 tsp. baking soda
1 tsp. baking powder
1/2 tsp. salt
4 bananas, mashed
¾ cup white sugar
1 egg lightly beaten
1/3 cup butter, melted
1/3 cup packed brown sugar
1/8 cup all-purpose flour
1/8 tsp. ground cinnamon
1 Tbsp. butter

Preheat oven to 375 degrees. Lightly grease 10 muffin cups. In a large bowl, mix together flour, baking soda, baking powder and salt. In another bowl, beat together bananas, sugar, egg and melted butter. Stir the banana mixture into the flour mixture just until moistened. Spoon batter into prepared muffin cups. In a small bowl, mix together brown sugar, flour and cinnamon. Cut in butter until mixture looks like cornmeal. Sprinkle topping over muffins. Bake for 18 to 20 minutes, until a toothpick inserted into center of a muffin comes out clean.

BLUEBERRY MUFFINS

1 ½ cups all-purpose flour
2 tsp. baking powder
½ tsp. salt
2 eggs
½ c. skim milk 2 Tbsp. vegetable oil

½ tsp. Vanilla extract

1 c. frozen blueberries, thawed and juices reserved

Preheat oven to 400 degrees. Combine the flour, baking powder, and salt in a mixing bowl. In a separate bowl, beat together the eggs, milk, oil, vanilla, and about 1/2 cup of the reserved blueberry juice. Add this mixture along with the blueberries to the dry ingredients and mix until thoroughly combined. Fill muffin tins about 2/3 full with the batter and bake for 20 to 25 minutes.

BREAD PUDDING

1 loaf of stale bread

1 qt. milk

½ c. butter

2 c. sugar

4 eggs beaten

1 Tbsp. vanilla

½ tsp. cinnamon

¼ tsp. nutmeg

1 c. diced & peeled apples

1 c. raisins

Crisco to grease pan

Preheat oven to 350 degrees. In a large bowl put bread crumbs in. In another bowl mix butter, sugar and eggs together. Add milk. Stir well. Add remaining ingredients. Mix everything together and pour over bread. Let stand until bread absorbs the mixture. Grease the baking dish. Pour into baking dish. Bake for 35-45 minutes. Serve with a rum or whiskey sauce on top.

WHISKEY SAUCE

2 eggs, beaten_

1 c. of confectioners **or** granulated sugar
1 c. heavy cream
¼ c. butter, melted
¼ c. Jack Daniel's

In a small saucepan, add eggs and whiskey or rum. Place over low heat. In a separate bowl, mix butter and sugar together. Pour slowly into eggs and liquor mixture. Stir well. Remove from heat and fold in cream. Pour over warm bread, and serve. Sauce may be refrigerated if not ready to use.

BREAKFAST BREAD

2 c. Flour
1 Tsp. Salt
2 Tbsp. Brown sugar
¾ cup Milk
1 Tbsp. Cinnamon
2 Tbsp. Melted butter
3 Apples, peeled and cored
4 tsp. Baking powder
4 Tbsp. Shortening
2 c. Chopped Raisins
1 Egg, Well beaten
2 Tbsp. Brown sugar

Preheat oven to 400 degrees. Sift flour, baking powder, salt, and sugar. Cut in shortening and add raisins. Add milk then egg to make a stiff dough. Mix thoroughly. Pour into well-oiled shallow pan. Brush dough with melted butter. Quarter apples and cut into thin slices. Arrange in rows in the dough, allowing edges to overlap. Brush apples with more melted butter and sprinkle with cinnamon and brown sugar. Bake 20 minutes or until apples are tender.

CORN BREAD

1 c. Self- rising flour

1 c. Corn meal

½ c. sugar

¾ stick melted butter

1 to 1 ½ cup milk

2 eggs beaten

Pre heat oven to 375.

In a cast iron skillet place butter in it and put it in the oven to melt butter. In a large bowl put flour, corn meal, sugar, eggs, and milk stirring well. Mixture should be about the consistency of cake mix but a little thicker. Pour the butter from skillet into the mixture and stir. Pour mixture back into the cast iron skillet. Bake for 45 minutes to 1 hour depending on your oven until done and golden brown.

GRAND MA ROSA'S 60 MINUTE ROLLS

1 1/2 cup warm milk

1 package dry yeast

3 Tbsp. shortening

1 tsp. salt

1 egg beaten

2 Tbsp. sugar

¾ cup instant potato flakes

4 cups flour

Preheat oven to 400 degrees. Add yeast, shortening, and sugar to milk. Stir well. Mix in egg, add flour, salt and potato flakes. Let rise 15 minutes, work down with a spoon and let it rise 15 more minutes. Shape into rolls and place in a greased pan or muffin pan. Let rise 15 minutes. Bake for 15 minutes or until done.

GRAND MA ROSA'S DINNER ROLLS

1 cup milk

1 Tbsp. Sugar

2 Tbsp. Butter

¾ tsp. salt

1 package active dry yeast

2 Tbsp. lukewarm water

1 egg

2 ½ to 3 ½ cups flour

Melted butter for brushing on top

Scald milk. Add sugar, butter and salt and stir until dissolved. Sprinkle yeast over warm water and let proof. When milk mixture has cooled to lukewarm, add to yeast mixture. Beat in egg. Stir in part of the flour; knead in the rest. Sprinkle enough flour to handle dough easily. Place in a greased bowl. Brush top with butter, and cover. Let the dough rise in a warm place until doubled in size (about 1 ½ hours). Punch down and roll into 2 inch pieces. Place rolls next to one another in rows about 1 inch apart on an un-greased baking sheet. Let rise a second time until light, about 35 minutes. Brush with melted butter and bake at 425 degrees for 20 minutes or until brown.

**Tip: Make sure you check the expiration date on yeast package and do not make the water boiling hot. **

GRAND MA ROSA'S SPOON BREAD

1 box corn muffin mix

1 can cream corn (small can)

2 eggs separate

1 8 oz. sour cream

1 stick butter

Melt butter in cast iron skillet (small). In a bowl add muffin mix, cream corn, sour cream, butter and egg yolks. Beat egg whites stiff fold in. Pour into pan. Bake at 425 degrees. 40-45 minutes.

JOHNNY CAKES

¾ cup cornmeal

1 egg, beaten

5 tsp. baking powder

1/3 cup sugar

2 Tbsp. vegetable oil

1 cup milk

1 tsp. nutmeg

Salt and pepper to taste

Preheat oven to 350 degrees. Mix all dry ingredients together in a bowl. Mix egg, milk and oil to dry mixture and mix well. Pour into a square baking pan and bake for 30-35 minutes.

PUMPKIN SPICE BREAD

1 can pumpkin (pureed)

1 cup vegetable oil

2/3 c. water

3 c. white sugar

3 ½ c. all-purpose flour

2 tsp. baking soda

1 tsp. salt

1 ½ tsp. ground cinnamon

1 tsp. ground nutmeg

½ tsp. ground cloves

¼ tsp. ground ginger

Preheat oven to 350 degrees. Grease and flour 3 loaf pans. In a large bowl, mix together pumpkin puree, eggs, oil, water and sugar. In a separate bowl, whisk together flour, baking soda, salt, cinnamon, nutmeg, cloves and ginger. Stir the dry ingredients into the pumpkin mixture until just blended. Pour into the prepared pans. Bake for 45 minutes.

(Loaves are done when toothpick inserted in center comes out clean.)

PUMPKIN SPICE MUFFINS

2/3 c. nonfat dry milk
6 Tbsp. flour
1 tsp. baking soda
¼ c. sugar substitute
2 tsp. pumpkin pie spice
1 tsp. cinnamon
2 eggs
1 c. canned pumpkin
1 tsp. vanilla
½ c. grated carrots or zucchini
4 Tbsp. raisins

Preheat oven to 350 degrees. Combine sifted dry ingredients in large mixing bowl and combine wet ingredients in a separate bowl. Mix just until everything is incorporated - batter should be lumpy. (Over mixing can cause muffins to be tough.) Bake for 20 minutes .

SWEET POTATO BREAD

1 ½ c. all- purpose flour
2 tsp. baking powder

¼ tsp. salt

1 tsp. ground nutmeg

½ tsp. ground cinnamon

1 c. white sugar

2 eggs (beaten)

½ c. vegetable oil

2 Tbsp. milk

1 c. sweet potatoes (cooked and mashed)

½ c. pecans (chopped)

Preheat oven to 325 degrees. Grease and 8x4 loaf pan. In a medium bowl, stir together the flour, baking powder, salt, nutmeg, cinnamon, and sugar. Add the eggs, oil and mixture. Mix well. Stir in the sweet potatoes and pecans. Pour batter in the loaf pan. Bake for 1 hour and 10 minutes, or until a toothpick comes out clean. Cool bread for 20 minutes before removing from pan.

SWEET POTATO CASSEROLE

6 Sweet potatoes (boiled until done)

1 stick butter melted

½ cup of brown sugar and white sugar

1/8 tsp. nutmeg

1 Tbsp. Cinnamon

2 eggs beaten

2 Tbsp. milk

Splenda to taste (optional)

Grease a casserole dish with cooking spray. Mix all ingredients with potatoes. Bake 350 degrees until top starts to brown.

***TIP: If you add 2 tsp. of flour to mixture this dish will now become a soufflé.

If you use Splenda you may want to leave out the brown sugar and white sugar. You may also use Splenda brown sugar(but remember to only use ½ of brown sugar measurement. Splenda brown sugar is extremely sweet) ***

Notes

Chapter 5

BREAST, THIGHS, LEGS, & BUTT
(Meats)

Baked Bar B Que Chicken

Beef Stir Fry

Beer & Herb Shrimp

Buffalo Wings

Chicken and Rice

Chili with a Kick

Grilled Pork Tenderloin

Lamb Chops

Lime and Coconut Chicken

Marinated Ribs in Beer

Nutty Sweet Pork Chops

Penne Pasta Alfredo

Pork Bar B Que

Raspberry Bar B Que Sauce

Salmon Croquettes

Shrimp Scampi

Stuffed Turkey Burgers

Beef or Turkey Sausage and Cabbage

Beef Stroganoff

Boneless Pork Tenderloin

Caprese Balsamic Chicken

Chicken Parmesan

Cornish Hens and Rice

Honey Chicken

Lemon Pepper fish

Mama's Fried Chicken

Meat Loaf

Pecan Chicken

Peppered Steak

Pork Roast

Rib Eye Steak

Sherry Chicken

Stuffed Cabbage Rolls

Tomato Chops

BAKED BAR B QUE CHICKEN

4 bone in chicken breast
2 eggs (scrambled)
½ c. water
2/3 c. milk
1 ½ Tbsp. salt
2 Tbsp. Black pepper
3 c. flour
1 Tbsp. garlic powder
1 ½ Tbsp. Mrs. Dash
1 small onion (sliced in rings)
Canola Oil
1 bottle of your favorite Bar B Que Sauce

In a bowl mix together eggs, water and milk. In a bag mix together all dry ingredients, dip chicken breast into egg mixture then in to dry ingredients. Put into canola oil. Make sure oil is hot. Brown chicken on both sides. Place into a baking dish and pour Bar B Que sauce over chicken, spread onions over chicken and bake at 300 degrees for 30 minutes. Bake covered. Pour your favorite sauce over chicken and bake for an additional 10 minutes.

BEEF or TURKEY SAUSAGE AND CABBAGE

1 medium head of cabbage
1 medium onion (sliced)
1 green pepper (sliced)
1 pkg. beef or Turkey Kielbasa sausage
2 strips of bacon (optional)
salt and pepper to taste
pinch of sugar

** If you do not use bacon use 1 Tbsp. butter to get the oil, you may also use turkey bacon to crumble in Cabbage**

Fry bacon in a pot that you are going to cook cabbage in. Cut up cabbage and place in pot with bacon and grease. Slice up onion and green pepper cook with cabbage. Salt and pepper to taste. Add the pinch of sugar and stir, mixing well. Once cabbage is almost completed cooking, cut sausage into 3 inch chunks. Place on top of cabbage. Cover and steam for 5-8 minutes. Serve with corn bread.

BEEF STIR FRY

5 Tbsp. dark soy sauce
8 Tbsp. Canola Oil
2 tsp. honey
2 tsp. Dijon mustard
½ tsp. red pepper flakes
1 lb. flank steak, cut into thin strips
2 cloves garlic, minced
2 tsp. fresh ginger, minced
1 medium onion, thinly sliced
1 red bell pepper, thinly sliced
1 green pepper, thinly sliced
1 bunch broccoli, cut into flowerets
1 can sliced water chestnuts
3 Tbsp. sesame seeds, toasted
Steamed rice as an accompaniment

Whisk together soy sauce, 4 tablespoons canola oil, honey, mustard and red pepper flakes, in a medium bowl. Add steak and toss. Marinate, covered at room temperature for 15 minutes. Heat 2 tablespoons canola oil over moderately high heat, in a wok or heavy skillet. Heat until the skillet is hot. Sauté garlic, ginger, onion, bell peppers and broccoli, stirring, 5-7 minutes. Transfer mixture to another bowl. Heat 2 tablespoons canola oil in wok over high heat until hot, but not smoking. Sauté steak, stirring about 2 minutes. Stir in sautéed vegetables, water chestnuts and sesame seed until heated through.

BEEF STROGANOFF

1 lb. Beef Stew cubes
½ tsp. garlic powder
½ tsp. salt
½ tsp. ground black pepper
1 cube beef bouillon
1 medium onion chopped
8 ounces fresh mushrooms (sliced)
1 pint sour cream
4 ounces egg noodles (cooked and drained)

In a large skillet, brown beef in oil over medium high heat. When meat is browned, drain excess fat from skillet. Add garlic powder, salt and pepper and stir in. Add bouillon, onion and mushrooms to skillet and sauté until onions are translucent. Remove from heat (very important) and add sour cream. Stir all together and serve over hot cooked egg noodles.

BEER & HERB SHRIMP

3 ½ lb. peeled large raw shrimp
2 c. dark beer
3½ Tbsp. garlic, minced
2½ Tbsp. chives, snipped
1 Tbsp. parsley, snipped

1 tsp. Old bay
1 tsp. salt
1 tsp. Pepper

Combine all ingredients in a gallon freezer bag except shrimp. Separate ¼ cup of the marinade and put into a sandwich bag. Add shrimp to the freezer bag. Seal and shake. Refrigerate overnight; turning bag occasionally. Broil shrimp 4 inches from heat until cooked, tender and pink. (about 3 minutes on each side) Do not overcook or shrimp will become tough. Brush occasionally with marinade. Serve shrimp on a bed of rice or pasta.

Note: You may also cook this on the grill.

BONELESS PORK TENDERLOIN

8 boneless pork tenderloin chops, 1/2-inch thick
1 c. thick and chunky hot salsa
6 Tbsp. water
6 Tbsp. orange marmalade
2 tsp. seasoned salt
1 tsp. garlic (minced)

In small bowl, combine salsa, water, marmalade and seasoned salt; blend well. Place pork chops in plastic freezer bag. Separate marinade. Pour 1/2 of marinade mixture over pork, turning to coat. Seal bag; marinate about 1 hour, turning pork chops several times. When ready to barbecue, remove pork chops from marinade and discard used marinade. Place chops on grill 4-6 inches above medium-high coals. Grill about 6 minutes per side, basting with reserved marinade.

BOURBON PECAN SALMON

4 Salmon Fillet
4 Tbsp. butter
½ c. Brown Sugar
½ c. chopped Pecans
1 cup bourbon (Jack Daniels)

In a skillet on medium heat, melt butter add brown sugar and stir until mixed well. Add pecans and coat well. Place salmon skin side down on top of the pecans and cook for 3 minutes. Flip the salmon and cook on that side for 3 more minutes. Pour bourbon over salmon and in the pan, stirring and spoon on top of the salmon. Cover and cook for 3 more minutes. Serve with rice pilaf.

BUFFALO WINGS

1 bag of wing dings (cleaned and washed)

1 Tbsp. Season Salt

1 Tbsp. Garlic Powder

1 Tbsp. Mrs. Dash seasoning Blend

½ tsp. Cajun seasoning

2 cups Self- rising flour

½ bottle to ¾ bottle Franks hot sauce (12 oz. bottle)

1 stick of butter

1 Tbsp. honey

Canola Oil

Heat Oil in a deep pot on medium heat.

In a bag add flour, season salt, garlic powder, Mrs. Dash, Cajun seasoning. Shake well. Season wings with same seasonings that you added to flour. Add wings to flour mixture. Coat well. Fry wings until golden brown.

In a separate pot, melt butter and add hot sauce and honey on low heat. Stir well. After wings are done place in a baking pan and pour hot sauce mixture over wings. Place in oven and bake at 350 degrees for 10 minutes.

CAPRESE BALSAMIC CHICKEN

6 Chicken Breast

4 tsp. season salt

2 tsp. Italian seasoning

1 ½ tsp. Garlic powder

1 tsp. Black pepper

1 package of sliced Mozzarella cheese

1 jar sun dried tomatoes in oil

1 package of basil leaves (fresh)

2/3 c. Balsamic vinegar

5 Tbsp. Brown sugar

1 tsp. minced garlic

1 Tbsp. Olive oil

1 Tbsp. sun dried Tomato oil

Clean and pocket chicken breast. Season chicken in the pocket and on both sides of chicken breast with Italian seasoning, garlic powder, season salt and black pepper. Open the pocket and place a slice of cheese, topped with sun dried tomato and basil leaves. Close chicken breast with tooth picks. In a cast iron skillet heat Olive oil and sun-dried tomato oil. Place chicken breast in skillet and cook each side for 5 minutes. While chicken is cooking, in a bowl mix vinegar, minced garlic and brown sugar. After turning the chicken and cooking it on the other side pour balsamic mixture over the chicken and cook until mixture start to thicken. Place in a 350 degree oven and bake for 20-25 minutes.

CHICKEN AND RICE

1 pound boneless skinless chicken breast

2 tablespoons butter

½ c. chopped mushrooms

1 onion, finely chopped

2 cloves garlic, minced

1 Tbsp. corn starch

1 c. long grain rice

2 ¼ c. milk

2 c. diagonally cut carrots

1 green pepper (cut in strips)

1 red pepper (cut in strips)

1 tsp. salt

½ tsp. pepper

Cut chicken into 1-inch cubes. In a large frying pan, cook chicken in butter over medium heat until chicken is lightly browned on all sides. Add mushrooms, onion and garlic; cook until onions are soft. Add corn starch, rice and cook for 2 min. Stir in milk, carrots, pepper strips, salt and pepper. Bring to a boil. Reduce heat to medium low, cover and simmer for 20 to 25 min, stirring occasionally.

CHICKEN PARMESAN

4 Boneless skinless chicken breast
Garlic Powder
Sea Salt
White Pepper
Italian Bread Crumbs
Parmesan Cheese
Mozzarella Cheese
¼ cup Olive oil
1 Jar or can of your favorite Spaghetti Sauce

Rinse chicken breast and set on a piece of wax paper. Season on both sides with the next 3 ingredients. In a freezer bag, put 1 ½ cups bread crumbs and ¼ cup of parmesan cheese and shake well. Add the chicken to the bag and coat well. In a skillet, heat olive oil. Brown breast on both sides. Pour spaghetti sauce in a 9X13 casserole dish. Put the browned breast on top of the sauce. Sprinkle with parmesan cheese and cover with foil. Bake at 350 for 40 minutes. Remove from oven and remove foil. Place a slice of mozzarella cheese on top of each breast cover again with foil and let it just rest on top of the stove.

CHILI WITH A KICK

1 lb. Ground Chuck
2 pounds round steak (cut into cubes)
1 teaspoon meat tenderizer
1 onion 1 Jalapeno pepper (finely chopped)
2 Tbsp. garlic, minced
3 Tbsp. distilled white vinegar
1 Tbsp. vegetable oil
3 Tbsp. Worcestershire sauce

4 tsp. chili powder

1-16 oz. can tomato sauce

2 cans Kidney beans **&** 1 can Chili beans

3 Tbsp. brown sugar

1 tsp. mustard powder

½ tsp. hot pepper sauce

Sprinkle round steak meat with meat tenderizer. Place in a 2 gallon freezer bag. Mix together onion, jalapeno pepper, garlic, vinegar, oil, Worcestershire sauce, and chili powder, and pour over steak. Marinate for 3 or more hours in the refrigerator. Remove cubed steak. (RESERVE MARINADE) In a small amount of oil, cook cubed round steak. Drain oil. Cook ground chuck. While meat is cooking prepare sauce. Combine reserved marinade, tomato sauce, brown sugar, mustard powder, Kidney beans, chili beans and hot sauce in a Dutch oven saucepan. Add steak and ground chuck. Simmer for 20 minutes over low heat or put into a crock pot and cook on low for 3 hours.

CORNISH HENS WITH RICE

1 c. Long grain rice

1 envelope savory herb and garlic soup mix

2 c. boiling water

1 can Cream of mushroom soup

2 Cornish hens Split

1 Tbsp. hot water

1 1/2 tsp. vegetable oil

Season Salt

Garlic Powder

Combine rice, mushroom soup, water, 1/2 of the soup mix. Pour into a 9 x 13 inch baking dish. Season hens and place on the rice mixture. Mix remaining soup mix, 1 Tbsp. hot water and 1 1/2 tsp. vegetable oil until blended. Brush evenly on skin side of the Cornish hens. Bake uncovered for 1 to 1 1/4 hours, at 350 degrees.

GRILLED PORK TENDERLOINS

½ c. Peanut oil

1/3 c. soy sauce

¼ c. red wine vinegar

3 Tbsp. lemon juice

2 Tbsp. Worcestershire sauce

3 Tbsp. minced garlic

1 Tbsp. chopped fresh parsley

1 Tbsp. dry mustard

1 ½ Tbsp. pepper

2 (3/4 - 1 lb.) Pork Tenderloins (sliced)

Combine first 9 ingredients, place in a shallow container or heavy duty zip top plastic bag. Add tenderloins, turning to coat. Cover or seal and chill 4 hrs., turning occasionally. Remove tenderloins from marinade & grill, covered 6 inches from medium coals (300 to 400 degrees) for 12 to 14 minutes or until done turning once.

HONEY CHICKEN
marinating required

4 lb. bag chicken wingettes or thighs

Season Salt

Garlic Powder

Black Pepper

2/3 cup honey

1/3 cup soy sauce

1 ½ Tbsp. Orange Marmalade

¼ cup Dijon-style mustard

3 Tbsp. vegetable oil

2 Tbsp. ginger, finely shredded

1 ½ tsp. finely shredded orange peel

Rinse chicken wingettes, or thighs. Place in 13 x 9 inch baking dish. Season chicken wings on both sides with season salt, garlic powder and black pepper – set aside. Combine remaining ingredients; mix well. Pour over chicken. Cover and refrigerate at least 6 hours or overnight. Place chicken and sauce in a single layer on foil-lined cookie sheet. Bake wings at 400 degrees 40 to 45 minutes or until well browned.(You may grill these wings, be careful, will burn easily because of the sugar content in the honey) Serve warm or at room temperature. You may use Ranch, Bleu Cheese or Picante Sauce to dip your chicken.

LAMB CHOPS

2-4 Lamb chops trimmed

Olive oil

Cajun Seasoning

Red Pepper flakes

Rosemary (dried)

Garlic Powder

Liquid Smoke

Butter (1 Tbsp. per chop)

Rub chops with olive oil on both sides. Put just a couple of shakes of Liquid smoke over chops. Season with Cajun season, red pepper flakes, rosemary, and garlic powder. Let it sit for 3 hours. (refrigerate). Melt butter in cast iron skillet and fry until desired doneness. Turn and cook the other side, **OR** you can sear it on both sides and place in oven to bake at 375 until it reaches desired doneness.

Tip: This recipe gives two ways to cook it

LEMON PEPPER FISH

1 ½ c. all-purpose flour

½ c. cornmeal

1 Tbsp. lemon pepper

4 eggs

6-8 fish fillets(Tilapia pictured)

¼ c. butter

½ c. peanut oil or Canola oil

Combine flour, cornmeal and lemon pepper. In a separate bowl, lightly beat eggs. In a large frying pan, melt butter over medium heat. One at a time, dip filets in egg and dredge in flour until well coated. Cook in hot butter and oil mixture, turning once, until brown on both sides.

LIME AND COCONUT CHICKEN

(grill or stove top recipe)

6 boneless skinless chicken breasts
4 Tbsp. oil
Zest of 1 lime
2 tsp. ground cumin
2 tsp. ground coriander
3 Tbsp. soy sauce
1 ½ tsp. kosher salt
2 ½ Tbsp. sugar
3 tsp. curry powder
1 cup coconut milk
pinch cayenne
½ cup chopped fresh cilantro
Fresh lime, cut into wedges (for garnish)

Trim fat from chicken breasts. Starting on thick side of the breasts slice the chicken breasts almost in half, then open each like a book. Put breast in between two pieces of wax paper and pound out until all breast are the same thickness. In a gallon freezer or storage bag mix remaining ingredients except fresh cilantro and limes. Add Chicken to marinade and chill. For 3 hours. Remove the breast from the marinade and pour marinade in a saucepan and bring to a boil for 3 minutes. Make sure you stir this, so it will not scorch or burn. to a rolling boil. Boil continuously for at least 2 minutes, stirring occasionally so it doesn't burn.

Place chicken in a cast iron skillet or grill. Heat a splash of oil over medium heat in the skillet. Do not over crowd the skillet. Cook each side about 5 minutes each. (By the chicken being thin it should not take long to cook)

Peirce the thickest part of chicken to make sure the juices run clear before you remove it from the skillet.

Sprinkle with fresh lime juice and sprinkle fresh Cilantro over the chicken. Serve with sauce on the side.

MAMA'S FRIED CHICKEN

1 Whole chicken cut up
Garlic Powder
Mrs. Dash
Season Salt
Pepper
Flour
½ tsp. Cajun seasoning
½ tsp. Creole seasoning
Canola oil or Peanut oil

Rinse chicken, lay out on a cookie sheet. Season chicken with the next 3 ingredients. In a separate bag mix flour, Cajun and Creole seasonings together. Coat chicken with flour mixture. Heat oil on medium heat. Add chicken slowly. Cook one side until chicken is a golden brown. Carefully turn chicken not to splash the oil. Cook on the opposite side. Turn one more time and when the juices running from the chicken is clear, the chicken is done. The chicken should be a golden brown. If you find that the chicken is cooking too fast lower the heat. If you cover the chicken while you are cooking it the coating will be soft, it will not be crispy. Do not cover after cooking, it also softens the coating.

MARINATED RIBS IN BEER

* requires overnight marinating*

2 slabs of ribs

3 Tbsp. Mrs. Dash (per slab)

3 Tbsp. season salt (per slab)

2 Tbsp. garlic powder (per slab)

1 Tbsp. savory (per slab)

1 Tbsp. marjoram (per slab)

1 Tbsp. Turmeric (per slab)

1 can beer (1/2 can per slab)

In a bowl mix all spices together. Place ribs in a rectangular baking dish or a deep aluminum pan. Pour beer over ribs. Sprinkle spices over both sides of ribs. Cover and refrigerate overnight. Grill or bake covered in the oven on 350 for 1 ½ hour.

MEAT LOAF

1 lb. ground turkey

1 pkg. hot Italian sausage

1 medium onion (chopped)

1 medium green pepper (chopped)

2 eggs (beaten)

¼ c. Cracker crumbs (saltine)

1 c. cream of mushroom soup

1 pkg. dry onion & mushroom soup

Sauté onion & pepper. Mix all ingredients together. Form a loaf and bake at 350 degrees for 1 hour 30 minutes.

NUTTY SWEET CHOPS

12 center cut pork chops

12 Tbsp. brown sugar

1¼ stick butter
Soy sauce
½ c. chopped pecans (optional)

Preheat oven to 350 degrees. Sprinkle each chop with soy sauce. Add 1 Tbsp. butter to each chop. Sprinkle with a Tbsp. brown sugar. Sprinkle with pecans, cover and bake for 45-50 minute

PECAN CHICKEN

6 boneless, skinless chicken breasts, pounded thin
4 cups ice water and ice
4 tsp. salt
3/4 c. ground pecans
2 whole eggs
2 Tbsp. milk
2 Tbsp. honey
½ tsp. salt
½ tsp. black pepper, course ground fresh

Marinate the chicken breasts in iced salt water for 1/2 hour. Beat milk with honey, then add beaten eggs, salt and fresh ground pepper. Put egg wash in one shallow bowl, and pecan meal in another. Dip each chicken breast in the egg wash, then into the pecan meal and pat the meal into the breast to form a crust. Place the breasts in a shallow baking pan; that has been sprayed with cooking spray, and bake for 35 minutes at 375, or until the breasts are done through.

PENNE PASTA ALFREDO

1 box of penne pasta
2 Tbsp. Olive oil

4 chicken breast (cubed) (optional)
4 Italian sausages (cubed) (optional)
½ lb. shrimp (peeled and deveined) (optional)
1 box broccoli (chopped)
2 pkg. Alfredo sauce
2 c. milk
6 Tbsp. butter

Boil pasta in Dutch oven pot. In a skillet add olive oil and sauté chicken. Remove chicken and cook sausage. Drain excess grease. Remove meat from skillet. Drain Pasta. In the Dutch oven pot, melt butter and add milk. Stir in Alfredo sauce and broccoli. Add meat, shrimp and pasta. Stirring occasionally; on medium low heat. Follow cooking directions on package. Let dish sit for 5 minutes after cooking to thicken.

*** This recipe can be made vegetarian or with meat***

PEPPERED STEAKS

3 Tbsp. Canola oil
½ tsp. Paprika
½ tsp. Pepper
¼ tsp. salt
¼ tsp. garlic powder
¼ tsp. lemon pepper seasoning
1/8 tsp. oregano
1/8 tsp. crushed red pepper flakes
1/8 tsp. ground cumin
1/8 tsp. cayenne pepper
4 Steaks of your choice

In a bowl, combine the first 10 ingredients. Remove Mix well. Brush mixture over steak on both sides and refrigerate for 1 hour. Grill over medium hot coals for desired doneness. Baste occasionally.

PORK BARBECUE

1 Boston butt (baked, then pulled or chopped)
2 Tbsp. brown sugar
2 Tbsp. all-purpose flour
2 Tbsp. dry mustard
2 tsp. salt
2 tsp. black pepper
2 tsp. paprika
2 tsp. cayenne pepper
2 tsp. garlic powder
2 tsp. chili powder
1/2 c. chopped onion
1 c. water
1 c. vinegar
1 c. broth from cooked meat
2 Tbsp. lemon juice
1 cup ketchup

Place roast in a pot. Cook thoroughly. Put all ingredients in a pot on low heat. Stirring occasionally for 30 minutes. Do not bring to a boil. When meat is finished cooking let cool and shred or cut into small cubes. Place meat into sauce and stir well. Heat thoroughly.

PORK ROAST

4 tsp. dried sage
4 tsp. dried thyme
4 tsp. dried rosemary
4 tsp. crushed marjoram

1 Boneless pork butt
1 red onion - cut into 1 inch chunks
1 c. apple juice
½ c. maple syrup

Combine the sage, thyme, rosemary, marjoram, salt and pepper. Rub over roast. Cover and refrigerate roast overnight. Preheat oven to 325 degrees. Place roast in a shallow roasting pan and bake for 2 ½ to 3 hours. Drain fat. The internal temperature of the roast is 145 degrees. Transfer the roast, to a serving platter and keep warm.. Skim excess fat from meat juices. Pour drippings into a heavy skillet. Stir in apple juice and syrup. Cook and stir over medium-high heat until liquid has been reduced by half, about 1 cup. Pour over sliced roast.

RASPBERRY BAR B QUE SAUCE

2- 12oz. jar raspberry preserves (seedless)
6 Tbsp. Red Wine Vinegar
1 cup Catsup
2 tsp. Chili Powder
2 tsp. Dijon Mustard
2 tsp. Cayenne Pepper (start with one and adjust to taste)

Bring to boil while stirring and then simmer for about 20 min. Stirring frequently. Reheat in microwave to bring back full flavor.

RIB EYE STEAK
* requires overnight marinating *

1 c. orange juice
½ c. Italian salad dressing

1 c. Worcestershire sauce

2 Tbsp. vinegar-based hot pepper sauce

2 Tbsp. minced fresh garlic

4- 1 ½ inch thick rib-eye steaks

salt and pepper to taste

In a large plastic freezer bag, combine the orange juice, salad dressing, Worcestershire sauce, hot pepper sauce, and garlic. Squeeze the bag to mix well. Place steaks into the bag with the marinade, and seal. Refrigerate overnight. Preheat an outdoor. When the grill is hot, lightly oil the rack. Place steaks onto the grill and season the tops with salt and pepper to taste. Baste with marinade. Cook for about 7 minutes, then flip over and salt, pepper and baste again. Grill for about 8 more minutes, or to desired doneness. Do not flip the steaks again. Let steaks stand for 5 minutes. Heat the remaining marinade to a boil in a small saucepan. Pour remaining marinade over steaks and place into a 250 degree oven to keep warm until ready to eat.

SALMON CROQUETTES

2 cans pink salmon

½ green pepper (chopped)

1 medium onion (chopped)

1 c. cracker crumbs

2 eggs, beaten

1 Tbsp. dried parsley

1 tsp. dry mustard

vegetable oil

Drain the salmon. Flake the meat; make sure you pick out the bones. In a medium bowl, combine the onions and green pepper with the salmon, ½ of the cracker crumbs, eggs, parsley, mustard and salmon. Mix well, shape into patties. Coat patties in remaining cracker crumbs. Melt shortening in a large skillet over medium heat. Cook patties until browned, then carefully turn and brown on the other side.

SHERRY CHICKEN

6 pieces of your favorite part of chicken
1 can cream of mushroom soup
1 ¼ cup cream sherry
8 oz. container of sour cream
Garlic powder
Mrs. Dash
Crushed red pepper
Cajun seasoning

Season chicken, with garlic powder, Mrs. Dash, Crushed red pepper, and Cajun Seasoning. Place in Refrigerator for at least 20 minutes.

In a separate bowl mix soup, sherry , and sour cream. Pour mixture over chicken and bake uncovered at 350 for 45 minutes or until chicken is completely done.

SHRIMP SCAMPI

1 ½ lb. shrimp (peeled and deveined)
½ lb. scallops
2 c. white wine
½ can beer
1 stick butter (melted)
1 Tbsp. minced garlic
1 Tbsp. Hot sauce
Mrs. Dash
Season Salt

Put wine, beer, butter, garlic, hot sauce, Mrs. Dash, and season salt in a freezer bag. Add shrimp and scallops. Refrigerate for 1-2 hours. Remove and put in a 9x13 casserole dish and bake at 350 for 20 minutes.

STUFFED CABBAGE ROLLS

1 head of cabbage
1 lb. ground beef
1 lb. ground turkey
1 c. rice (cooked)
1 carrots (chopped)
1 onion (chopped)
1 green pepper (chopped)
1 can of Diced Tomatoes
Sea Salt
White Pepper
Garlic Powder
Vinegar

Combine all ingredients together <u>except</u> cabbage, diced tomatoes and vinegar.

Blanche cabbage leaves, roll meat mixture in the leaves. Put rolls in a casserole dish. Salt and pepper rolls. Sprinkle vinegar over the rolls. Cover with diced tomatoes. Cover with lid and bake at 350 for 1 ½ hours.

** You may use all ground turkey or all ground beef if you wish**

STUFFED TURKEY BURGERS

2 lbs. ground turkey meat
2 Tbsp. Worcestershire sauce
1 tsp. minced garlic
2 ½ Tbsp. Mrs. Dash
1 ½ Tbsp. Season Salt
1 small onion (chopped)
1 egg (scrambled)
Feta Cheese
Mushrooms (chopped)

In a large bowl mix the first 7 ingredients well. Make patties. Top one patty with feta cheese and chopped mushrooms. Cover with another patty and squeeze together the edges. Place on a hot grill. Turn when the first side is done.

TOMATO CHOPS

6-8 pork chops
1 large onion (sliced)
1 green pepper (sliced)
2 Tbsp. season salt
2 Tbsp. Mrs. Dash
1 tsp. garlic powder
1 can tomato soup

In a baking dish, place chops in dish. Combine season salt, Mrs. Dash, & garlic powder together. Sprinkle over both sides of chops. Slice onion and pepper up over chops. Pour tomato soup over chops. <u>Do not</u> <u>mix soup with water</u>. Top with sliced onion and green pepper. Cover and bake at 325 degrees for 45 minutes to 1 hour.

Notes

Chapter 6

THE BIG "O"
(Desserts)

Apple Cake

Apple Crumb Pie

Banana Pudding

Better than Sex Cake

Butterscotch Nut Bars

Carrot Cake

Chocolate Brownies

Cream Cheese Pound Cake

Fried Bananas

Icing

Low Fat Cheesecake

Pineapple Upside Down Cake

Pumpkin Pie

Strawberry Daiquiri Pie

Sweet Potato Pie

Triple Nut Brownies

Apple Cinnamon Crisp

Apple Tarts

Banana Split Cake

Blueberry Cobbler

Caramel Corn

Cherry Apple Dump Cake

Chocolate Butter Cream Frosting

Diabetic Carrot Cake

Grand Daddy Hubert's Chocolate Cake

Lemon Bars

Oatmeal Raisin Cookies

Pound Cake

Rum Cake

Strawberry Short Cake

Tiramisu Cheese Cake

Turtle Cheese Cake

APPLE CAKE

2 ½ c. all-purpose flour
1 c. sugar
1 tsp. baking soda
2 ¼ tsp. cinnamon
¼ tsp. ground nutmeg
1/8 tsp. mace
1 egg
1 tsp. Vanilla
½ c. applesauce
½ c. buttermilk
1 ½ c. tart apples; diced
½ c. raisins
brown sugar

Preheat oven to 350 degrees. Sift together flour, sugar, baking soda and spices. In mixer bowl put egg, vanilla, apple sauce and milk. Mix well. Gradually add dry ingredients, blending well. Fold in apples and raisins by hand. Spray an 8x8 pan with cooking spray. Pour batter into pan. Sprinkle with brown sugar. Bake for 55 minutes.

APPLE CINNAMON CRISP

11 medium sized apples (Fuji)
2 ½ teaspoons cinnamon

Topping:
1¾ c. flour
1c.brown sugar
½ c. butter

Syrup:
1 cup brown sugar
1/4 cup hot water
Juice of ½ lemon

Peel, core and slice apples in eighths. Spread them over the bottom of a lightly greased 9 x 12 inch baking pan. Sprinkle cinnamon over the apples. To make topping, mix the flour and 1cup brown sugar together, cut in the butter until crumbly. Set aside.

Syrup: Mix 1 cup brown sugar with the hot water and lemon juice. Pour half of the syrup over the apples. Sprinkle the topping mixture evenly over top. Pour the remaining syrup over the topping. Bake at 350 degrees 60 minutes.

> ****TIP:** If you cannot find Fuji apples, here are some other apples that will work just as well. Gala, Rome, Gold Rush, Cortland, Granny Smith, or Jonathan. Granny smith apples are a little tart. ******

APPLE CRUMB PIE

4 gala apples
½ c. sugar
1 teaspoon cinnamon
1 prepackaged pie shell, thawed

Crumb topping:
½ c. sugar
¾ c. flour
1/3 c. butter

Cut apples in 1/8 and arrange in a pastry lined pan. Mix the 1/2 cup of sugar with the cinnamon. Sprinkle over the apples. Mix all topping ingredients together until crumbly and spread out over the apples. Bake at 400 degrees for 40-50 min.

APPLE TART

1 prepackaged pie crust
1 egg yolk
2 oz. Water
2 lbs. Apples, sweet red
2 ½ Tbsp. Lemon juice
3 Eggs, beaten
½ c. Sugar
½ c. Cream
½ tsp. Vanilla

Take prepackaged pie crust and roll out on a floured board. Place in a large shallow pie pan or spring-form pan. Peel, core and thinly slice the apples. Toss in lemon juice. Arrange a layer on the crust. Mix together the beaten eggs, 1/2 cup sugar, cream and vanilla. Pour over the apples. Bake at 400 for 20 minutes. Reduce the heat to 350 and bake for 20 minutes longer (or until the filling is firm).

BANANA PUDDING

(This is Eric's favorite dessert)

1 large package instant vanilla pudding mix
1 1/2 c. cold milk
1 1/2 c. half and half
1 small container sour cream
1 Tbsp. vanilla extract
Cinnamon

Nutmeg

1 container frozen whipped topping, thawed

1 package vanilla wafers

7 bananas (sliced)

1 In a large mixing bowl, beat pudding mix and milk for 2 minutes. Stir in vanilla and fold in whipped topping and sour cream. Layer wafers, bananas and pudding mixture and sprinkle with cinnamon and nutmeg, repeat for each layer. Ending with crumbled remaining cookie wafers.

**Tip: Go light on the nutmeg, it has an over powering flavor with this recipe.

PINEAPPLE STRAWBERRY BANANA SPLIT CAKE

(Made this on Charlotte Today)

1 stick butter

2 ½ cups graham cracker crumbs

½ c. sugar

3 cups confectioner's sugar

1 8-oz. package cream cheese, softened

1/3 c. milk

15-oz.can crushed pineapple

1 cup cool whip

1 pint of strawberries quartered (optional)

1 bottle chocolate syrup

8 bananas quartered

1 jar Maraschino Cherries

1-2 c. chopped pecans

Melt butter in the microwave. In a bowl pour the butter and stir in graham cracker crumbs and sugar. Spread graham cracker mixture to make crust. Bake for about 5 minutes at 250 degrees. Set aside to cool. Prepare the second layer by combining confectioner's sugar, cream cheese & milk. Spread over graham cracker crust. Next layer consist of pineapple. The next layer is bananas. Next you fill in with the strawberries. The next layer is cool whip topping. Drizzle the chocolate syrup over the cool whip. Top with maraschino cherries & nuts. Refrigerate to set.

BETTER THAN SEX CAKE

1 German chocolate cake mix
1 can sweetened and condensed milk (I use Eagle brand)
1 jar caramel ice cream topping
1 8 ounce container of Cool Whip
6 ounces crushed Heath bar
6 ounces crushed plain Hershey bar

Bake cake as directed in 9x13 pan. Take the handle of a wooden spoon and poke holes all over the cake while it's still warm. Pour can of condensed milk over warm cake, then repeat with caramel topping. Refrigerate for 6 hours. Frost cake with Cool Whip topping and sprinkle with crushed Heath & Hershey bar.

BLUEBERRY COBBLER
(you may use peaches or strawberries as a substitute)

6 cups fresh or frozen (thawed) blueberries
3 Tbsp. cornstarch
1/3 c. sugar
1 Tbsp. frozen orange juice concentrate, thawed
1/3 c. oat bran
2/3 c. all-purpose flour

¼ c. sugar

1 ½ tsp. Baking powder

½ c. buttermilk

Coat a 2 ½ quart casserole dish with nonstick cooking spray. Combine the filling ingredients in a medium-sized bowl, and set aside for 15 minutes to allow the juices to develop. Then stir gently to mix well, and transfer to the prepared dish. Combine all of the topping ingredients except for the buttermilk in a medium-sized bowl, and stir to mix well. Add the buttermilk, and stir just until the dry ingredients are moistened. Drop heaping tablespoonfuls of the batter onto the blueberry mixture to make 8 biscuits. Bake at 375 degrees for about 45 minutes, or until the filling is bubbly and the topping is golden brown. If the topping starts to brown too quickly, cover the dish loosely with aluminum foil during the last 10 minutes of baking. Remove the cobbler from the oven, and let it sit for 10 minutes.

BUTTERSCOTCH NUT BARS

2 ¼ c. Tbsp. butter

1 ½ c. brown sugar

4 Tbsp. white sugar

5 c. all-purpose flour

2 ½ tsp. salt

2 packages butterscotch chips

1 ¼ c. light corn syrup

½ c. water

6 Tbsp. butter

3 ½ c. salted cashew halves

In a mixing bowl, cream the butter and sugar. Combine flour and salt; add to creamed mixture just until combined. Press into 2 greased 9x13 baking pan. Bake at 350 degrees until lightly browned. Combine butterscotch chips, corn syrup, butter and water in sauce pan. Cook until chips and butter are melted. Spread over crust. Sprinkle with cashews; press down lightly. Bake for 11-13 minutes or until topping is bubbly and lightly browned.

CARAMEL CORN

1 cup butter
2 cup brown sugar
1/2 cup corn syrup
1 tsp. salt
1 tsp. vanilla
1 tsp. baking soda
6 quarts popped, unflavored popcorn

Melt butter; stir in brown sugar, corn syrup, and salt. Bring to a boil, stirring constantly. Boil without stirring; 5 minutes. Remove from heat; stir in baking soda and vanilla. Gradually pour syrup mixture over popped corn, mixing well. Pour into 2 cookie sheets and bake in a 250 degree oven for 1 hour, stirring every 15 minutes. Remove from oven and cool completely.

CARROT CAKE

2 cups all-purpose flour

2 cups granulated sugar

1/2 teaspoon salt

2 tsp. ground cinnamon

1/2 tsp. ground nutmeg

3 eggs

1 1/2 cups vegetable oil

2 cups finely grated carrots (about 3 to 4 medium carrots)

2 teaspoons vanilla extract

1 can (8 or 12 ounces) well drained pineapple

 1/2 cup chopped walnuts, divided

In a mixing bowl, combine dry ingredients; stir to blend. Add eggs, oil, shredded carrots, and vanilla; beat until well blended. Stir in pineapple, and the walnuts. Pour into a greased and floured 13x9x2-inch baking pan. Bake at 350 degrees for 50 to 60 minutes, or until a wooden tooth pick or cake tester inserted in center comes out clean. Place cake in pan on a rack to cool. Let cool, icing recipe follows.

ICING

1 stick margarine (soft)

8 oz. cream cheese

2 tsp. Vanilla

1 lb. confectioner's sugar

Mix all ingredients together.

CHOCOLATE BROWNIES

½ c. cake flour, sifted

½ c. unsweetened cocoa powder

¼ tsp. salt

2 egg whites

1 large egg

¾ c. granulated sugar

6 Tbsp. unsweetened applesauce

2 Tbsp. Vegetable oil

1 ½ tsp. vanilla extract

Pre heat oven to 350 degrees. Spray an 8 - inch square baking pan with vegetable cooking spray and set aside. Combine flour, cocoa, and salt. Mix well. In a separate bowl , whisk together egg whites, egg, sugar, applesauce, oil, and vanilla. Stir in flour mixture until just blended; do not over mix. Pour batter into prepared pan. Bake until just set and a toothpick inserted in center comes out clean, about 25 minutes. Place pan on a wire rack and cool for at least 15 minutes. Cut brownies into squares and place on a serving plate.

CREAM CHEESE POUND CAKE

2 sticks butter soft (room temp)

3 c. sugar

Salt

1-8 oz. Neufchatel cheese

6 eggs

1 ½ tsp. Vanilla extract

1 tsp. Lemon extract

3 c. all-purpose flour

Cream butter, cheese and sugar until creamy. Add a pinch of salt, vanilla, and lemon extract. Mix well. Add eggs one at a time, alternating with flour. Pour mix in a Bundt pan. Bake at 325 for 1 ½ hours. Stick a toothpick in it. If it comes out clean the cake is done.

DIABETIC CARROT CAKE

Butter-flavored cooking spray or cooking spray for baking.

2 large egg whites, at room temperature

½ cup plain nonfat yogurt

3 Tbsp. canola oil

½ c. unsweetened applesauce

1/3 c. dark brown sugar, packed

2 tsp. vanilla extract

2 ½ c. unbleached all-purpose flour

2 tsp. baking powder

½ tsp. baking soda

¼ tsp. salt

1 tsp. ground cinnamon

½ tsp. ground nutmeg

1 c. shredded carrots

4 oz unsweetened crushed pineapple with juice

¼ c. dark raisins

Preheat the oven to 375 degrees. Position the top rack in the center of the oven. Lightly coat a 9 inch tube pan with cooking spray. Dust with flour and tap out excess. In a large bowl, whisk together the egg whites, yogurt, oil, applesauce, brown sugar, and vanilla. On a piece of waxed paper, sift together the flour, baking powder, baking soda, salt, cinnamon, and nutmeg. Gradually add to egg-applesauce mixture, stirring until well mixed. Stir in the carrots. Drain and reserve the juice from the pineapple. Stir the drained pineapple and raisins into the cake batter. Spoon the batter into the prepared pan, smoothing the top with the back of a spoon or spatula. Bake for 40 to 45 minutes. Cool in the pan on a rack for 10 minutes. Slide a thin knife around the edges and center of the cake to loosen it from the pan. Invert onto a rack to cool. When ready to serve, transfer cake to a serving platter.

>**Tip: If you are using cooking spray for baking, skip flouring the pan. To test cake for doneness, use a tooth pick. If it comes out clean it is done.

FRIED BANANAS

½ c. Flour

½ c. Water

½ tsp. Baking powder

1 Egg, lightly beaten

2 Bananas

¼ c. Cream

½ c. Brown sugar

2 tsp. Butter

1 Tbsp. Dark rum

Vanilla ice cream

Add the cream, sugar, butter and rum to a saucepan. Heat until just hot (do not boil). Set aside. Whisk together the flour, water, baking powder and egg. Peel the bananas. Split in half, length-wise. Heat about 1/2 -inch of oil in a skillet. Dip the banana in the batter, add to the hot oil and cook (turning once) until lightly browned (about 2 minutes per side). Drain on paper towels. Place the banana on 4 plates, add a scoop of ice cream and top with the rum sauce.

GRANDDADDY HUBERT'S FAVORITE CHOCOLATE CAKE

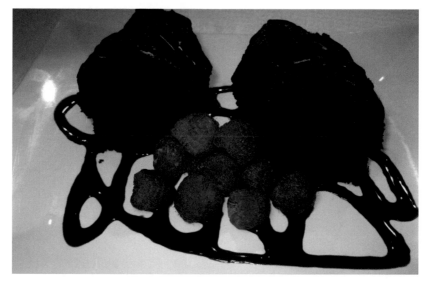

¾ c. Cocoa powder

¾ c. boiling water

¾ c. shortening

2 cups sugar

1 ½ tsp. vanilla extract

3 eggs

2 ¾ cup all-purpose flour

2 tsp. baking soda

½ tsp. salt

1 2/3 cups buttermilk

In a small bowl mix first two ingredients until smooth, set aside. Preheat oven to 350 degrees. Grease and flour 2 round 9 inch pans. In a large bowl cream next 3 ingredients together until fluffy. Add eggs one at a time. Beat well. Sift flour, baking soda and salt together; alternating with buttermilk to mixture in the large bowl. Mix until smooth. Blend in cocoa mixture. Pour into 9 inch pans bake 35-45 minutes depending on oven. Cool on rack before frosting. Use a Chocolate Butter Cream frosting.

CHOCOLATE BUTTER CREAM FROSTING

¾ c. butter softened

5 1/3 c. Confectioners' sugar

1 c. Cocoa Powder

2/3 c. Milk

2 tsp. Vanilla extract

Warm milk. In a bowl sift confectioner's sugar and cocoa powder. Add softened butter. Add milk a little at a time. Stirring until smooth. May need additional milk. Add vanilla and mix well.

LEMON BARS

1 c. butter
½ c. confectioner's sugar
2 cups all-purpose flour
½ tsp. salt
4 eggs, beaten until fluffy
2 cups sugar
5 Tbsp. lemon juice
2 Tbsp. grated lemon rind
Confectioner's sugar for topping

Preheat oven to 300. In a large bowl, cream together butter and confectioners' sugar; then blend in flour and salt. Press mixture down in a flat buttered cookie pan. Bake at 300 for 20 minutes. While crust is baking, in a medium bowl blend together eggs, sugar, lemon juice and rind. Pour over crust. Raise temperature to 350 and bake for an additional 15-20 minutes at 350. Remove from oven and let cool. When cooled, sprinkle generously with additional powdered sugar.

LOW FAT CHEESE CAKE
no baking required

1 Prepared graham cracker crust
2 c. low fat Cottage Cheese
1- 8 oz. container of cream cheese (low fat)
¼ c. orange juice
¼ tsp. salt
1 c. milk
3 egg yolks
2/3 c. sugar
2 tsp. vanilla
1 finely grated orange rind
¾ c. orange juice

2 envelopes unflavored gelatin

4 Tbsp. Low calorie strawberry jam

2 c. sliced fresh fruit (Kiwi, Strawberries, Blueberries, and Raspberries)

Place crust into refrigerator. In a food processor add first 3 ingredients blend for about 10 seconds or until cottage cheese is smooth. In a saucepan on low heat add next 4 ingredients. Stir on heat for about 4 minutes. Add orange rind and vanilla. Mix well. In a separate bowl mix orange juice and gelatin together. In a large bowl mix cheese mixture, gelatin mixture, and egg mixture. Stir well. Place into refrigerator for about 1 1/2 hours. Beat 3 egg whites into meringue. Fold into refrigerated mixture. Remove crust. Pour mixture into crust and refrigerate until firm about 2 hours. Spoon low-cal warm strawberry jam on top. Add sliced fruit on top.

OATMEAL RAISIN COOKIES

3 c. all-purpose flour

2 tsp. baking soda

½ tsp. salt

2/3 c. butter

2 c. dark brown sugar

2 c. granulated sugar

1c. Vegetable oil

4 eggs

2 tsp. vanilla

3 c. rolled oats

2 c. coconut (optional)

2 c. raisins

2 c. semisweet chocolate pieces

1 c. chopped walnuts

In a bowl, stir together flour, baking soda and salt, set aside. In a very large mixing bowl, beat butter with electric mixer 30 seconds. Beat in sugars, oil, eggs and vanilla. Add flour mixture, beat till well combined. Stir in rolled oats, coconut, raisins, chocolate pieces and walnuts. Drop by rounded teaspoons 2 inches apart on an un-greased cookie sheet. Bake in a 325 degree oven for 10 to 12 minutes or till edges are lightly browned.

PEACH APPLE DUMP CAKE

1 box yellow cake mix
1 can Peach pie filling
1 can apple pie filling
1 lg. can crushed pineapple (heavy syrup)
1 pkg. pecans (chopped)
1 stick butter

In a dish, lay out pineapple, on top add cherry and apple pie filling. DO NOT STIR. Pour DRY cake mix over pie filling. Cut each Tbsp. of butter into quarters, spread over top of cake mix. Sprinkle pecans over butter. REMEMBER: Do not stir. Cover and bake at 375 degrees for 1 hour. Uncover and bake for 30-40 minutes. Serve hot or cold with vanilla ice cream.

PINEAPPLE UPSIDE DOWN CAKE

1/3 c. butter
1 c. brown sugar
9 slices canned pineapple
9 maraschino cherries
1 ¾ c. flour
1 Tbsp. baking powder
½ tsp. salt
½ c. butter
1 c. white sugar

2 eggs

1 tsp. vanilla

¾ c. milk

Preheat oven to 350 degrees. Melt 1/3 cup of butter in a square cake pan in the oven and remove from heat. Sprinkling the brown sugar evenly. Arrange pineapple rings on top of the sugar, and put a cherry inside of each pineapple ring. In a small bowl, combine flour, baking powder and salt. In a separate bowl, cream remaining butter and sugar. Add eggs one at a time and continue beating until light. Stir in vanilla. Alternate additions of dry ingredients and milk to the creamed mixture. Pour over the pineapple in the square pan.

Bake for 55 minutes or until toothpick inserted comes out clean. Cool for 12 minutes. Turn upside down on a serving plate.

POUND CAKE

2 ¼ c. all-purpose flour

¾ tsp. baking powder

¼ tsp. baking soda

¼ tsp. salt

1/8 tsp. mace, ground

½ c. butter

1 cup sugar

3 egg whites

1 tsp. vanilla extract

½ tsp. lemon extract

¾ c. buttermilk

Preheat oven to 350 degrees. Spray an 8 1/2 by 4 1/2 inch loaf pan with nonstick cooking spray. In a bowl, combine flour, baking powder, baking soda, salt and mace. Mix well and set aside. In a mixing bowl, cream margarine and sugar together until smooth. Add egg whites and vanilla; blend until smooth. Alternately add flour mixture and buttermilk to batter in two additions each, blending well after each addition. Spoon batter into prepared pan and bake for 1 hour. Let cake cool before slicing.

PUMPKIN PIE

Crust:
1 c. Flour
¼ c. Brown Sugar
½ c. Chopped Pecans
½ c. Melted butter

Combine all ingredients and spread into a pie dish. Bake at 350 degrees for 20 minutes. Cool.

Filling
4 oz. cream cheese, softened
1 Tbsp. Half and Half
1 Tbsp. Sugar
1 ½ c. Thawed cool whip
1 c. half and half
2- 4oz. packages of Instant Vanilla Pudding
1 -16oz. can Pumpkin
1 tsp. cinnamon, ground
½ tsp. Ginger, ground
¼ tsp. Cloves, ground

Add first 3 ingredients in a large bowl and stir with wire whisk until smooth. Gently Stir In cool whip and spread on top of crust. Pour rest of the half and half into bowl with vanilla pudding and beat with wire Whisk until well blended (1 or 2 minutes, Mixture will be thick). Stir pumpkin and spices into Pudding mixture and mix well. Spread this over cream cheese layer and refrigerate at least 3 hours.

RUM CAKE

½ c. pecans
½ c. walnuts
1 box yellow cake mix
1 sm. Pkg. instant vanilla pudding mix
4 eggs
½ c. water
½ c. canola oil
½ c. spice rum
1 tsp. Vanilla extract

Glaze:
½ c. butter
¼ c. water
1 c. sugar
½ c. 151 rum <u>or</u> Spice Rum

Grease and flour a Bundt pan. Spread the nuts out evenly in the bottom of the pan. Mix together the pudding and cake mix adding eggs one at a time. Next add the water, oil, rum and vanilla extract. Mix until smooth. Pour batter over nuts. Bake for 50-60 minutes at 325 degrees. Use a toothpick to check for doneness.

For the glaze: In a small pot, melt butter, water, and sugar. Stirring all the time. When mixture starts to boil, stir until mixture is reduced about ½ . Remove it from the heat and add the rum. Stir Well.

Take the cake out of the pan and place on a plate. Use a toothpick and punch holes in the top of the cake to absorb the glaze mixture. Pour glaze mixture back into the pan. Put the cake back into the pan. Toothpick pricked side down. (Be careful it will splash) Let sit until cool. Turn back onto a plate to remove from pan.

STRAWBERRY DAIQUIRI PIE

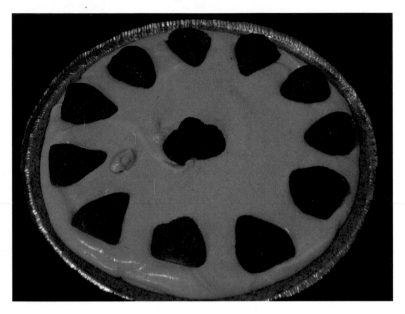

1 (10 inch) graham cracker crust

1(8 oz.) pkg. cream cheese, softened

1 can <u>sweetened</u> <u>condensed</u> milk

¾ cup to 1 cup strawberry daiquiri mix (bottled)
(if you use frozen in can, thaw first)

¼ c. chopped strawberries (optional)

3 Tbsp. light rum

1 tsp. lemon juice

4 oz. Whipping cream (cool whip in container)

Strawberries for garnish

In a large bowl, whip cream cheese until it is fluffy. Mix in condensed milk until mixture is smooth. Add daiquiri mix, lemon juice, and rum until creamy. Add whipping cream until all same color. Fold in strawberries. Pour into graham cracker crust and chill for 4-6 hours or until pie is firm.
Garnish as desired.

Tip: Make sure you use sweetened condensed milk NOT Evaporated milk

STRAWBERRY SHORTCAKE

4 c. flour

2 Tbsp. baking powder

½ c. sugar

1 ½ tsp. salt

1 lemon zest

½ tsp. nutmeg

8 Tbsp. cold butter cut into chips

2 c. buttermilk

3 pints strawberries, hulled and sliced

¼ c. fine sugar

1 pint heavy cream, whipped or whipped topping

Mix the berries with the sugar and allow to sit overnight to extract fresh strawberry juices. Combine all dry ingredients in the food processor. Pulse to combine. Add cold butter chips and pulse until the mixture resembles corn meal. Remove to a work bowl and add the buttermilk while mixing with hands until a sticky but firm dough forms. Line a baking sheet with parchment paper and spray with a non-stick spray. Make rough shape balls of dough. (3-4 inches in diameter.) Brush with buttermilk and sprinkle with sugar. Bake at 400 for about 20-25 minutes or until done. Split the biscuits and fill with strawberries and their juices. Top with whipped cream and the top half of biscuit.

***TIP: If you want to take the easy way out, use pre-packaged shortcakes. Pour strawberry mixture over the top with whipped topping.

SWEET POTATO PIE

6 Sweet Potatoes
2 Sticks Butter (melted)
2 Eggs (beaten)
1 tsp. Vanilla
1 c. sugar
1 c. brown sugar
1 tsp. Nutmeg
1 ½ tsp. Cinnamon
½ tsp. Allspice
2 Pie Crust (Frozen)

Brown Crust, Peel, cut up potatoes, boil until soft. Add butter. Mash up well. Stir in eggs. Add next7 ingredients. Taste using ¾ c. white and brown sugar first, If not sweet enough add the other ¼ cup of white and brown sugar. Add more sugar if needed if not sweet enough. Mix well, bake at 350 degrees until solid.

TIRAMISU CHEESECAKE

2 packages (8 ounces each) fat-free cream cheese
1 packages (4 ounces) sugar free instant vanilla pudding mix
2/3 c. dry milk powder
1 c. cold coffee (may use decaf)
1 tsp. Brandy extract
¾ c. Cool-Whip lite
1 prepared chocolate pie crust
2 Tbsp. unsweetened cocoa

In a large bowl, stir cream cheese with a spoon until soft. Add dry pudding mix, dry milk powder and coffee. Mix well using a wire whisk. Blend in brandy extract and 1/4 cup Cool Whip lite. Spread mixture into pie crust. Evenly drop the rest of the Cool Whip lite by tablespoon to form 8 mounds. Sprinkle chocolate chips over top. Refrigerate for at least 1 hour.

TRIPLE NUT BROWNIES

1 bag caramels
1/3 c. evaporated milk
8 oz. German sweet chocolate
6 Tbsp. butter
4 eggs
1 c. sugar
1 c. flour (sifted)
1 tsp. baking powder
½ tsp. salt
2 tsp. vanilla
8 oz. chocolate chips
1 c. chopped walnuts
1 c. chopped pecans
1 c. macadamia nuts

Preheat oven to 350 degrees. Grease and flour a 9 x 13 baking pan. Combine caramels and evaporated milk in top of double boiler over low heat. Cover and simmer until caramel is melted, stirring occasionally. Set aside, keeping warm. Combine German sweet chocolate and butter in 2 quart saucepan. Place over low heat stirring occasionally until melted. Remove from heat. Cool to room temperature. Beat eggs until foamy using electric mixer at high speed. Gradually add sugar, beating until mixture is thick and lemon colored. Sift together flour, Blend in cooled chocolate mixture and vanilla. Spread half of mixture into prepared baking pan. Bake for 6 minutes. Remove from oven and spread caramel mixture carefully over baked layer. Sprinkle with chocolate chips.

Stir ½ cup of walnuts & ½ c. of pecans, 1/2c macadamia nuts into remaining chocolate batter. Spread batter by spoonful over the caramel layer. Sprinkle with remaining nuts. Bake for 20 minutes

TURTLE CHEESE CAKE

3-8 oz. bricks Neufchatel Cheese (softened, room temp.)

1- 9" graham cracker crust or 9" chocolate crust

½ cup sugar

1 tsp. vanilla extract

1 Tbsp. lemon juice

2 eggs (beaten)

1 container caramel apple dip

1 container chocolate magic shell

1 small bag chopped pecans

In a large bowl, mix cheese, sugar, vanilla, lemon juice and eggs. Pour into the 9" graham cracker crust. Bake at 325 for 1 hour 15 minutes to 1 ½ hours. Check the center of cake with a toothpick. If it comes out clean the cake is done. While cheese cake is warm brush a layer of caramel apple dip over the top of the cheese cake. Let the cheese cake cool down. Add more caramel thick over the top. Drizzle magic shell and sprinkle with pecans.

> ** Tip: If you do not like chocolate, you may use strawberry jam instead.

Notes

Chapter 7

The Morning After

HAND SCRUB

1 slice of lemon

½ tsp sugar

Place in palm of your hand and rub together squeezing out all the lemon juice. Rinse hands with warm water.

FACIAL MASK

½ c. oatmeal

½ c. plain yogurt

3 drops of Tea tree oil

Stir together and put on face. Allow to dry a little and remove with warm water.

PUFFY EYES

Tea Bags

Place 2 tea bags in warm water, remove tea bags and allow to cool down . Place cooled bags over eyes and cover with a soft cloth for 12 minutes.

Cucumbers

Cut cucumbers into thick slices. Place in refrigerator for 15 to 20 minutes. Place cold cucumbers on eye lids for 12 minutes.

Water

Drink at least 8 to 10 glasses a day.

WELL BEING

- Slow Metabolism drink Green Tea
- Sleepless Nights drink Chamomile Tea
- Nauseous drink Ginger Tea
- Bloated drink Peppermint Tea

BENEFITS OF TURMERIC

- Natural anti inflammatory
- Natural antiseptic
- Improves digestion
- Anti-arthritic
- Helps prevent gas

FACIAL WASH

3 Tbsp. honey
1 Tbsp lemon juice
4 drops Tea Tree oil

Mix together in a bowl and refrigerate for 15 minutes. Remove and place on face and massage skin. Leave on for about 5 minutes and rinse with warm water.

SHAVING LEGS AND ARMS

- Be gentle
- Use shampoo or Shaving cream

- Use a clean razor (dull razor causes nicks)
- Longer strokes makes a better shave
- Moisturize legs and arms after shaving

Notes:

Chapter 8

SPICE IT UP

1. Start with a treasure hunt. Leave a note at the front door or the garage door along with a gift bag or basket to collect all the treasures that will be used during the evening. Place items throughout the house with instructions to go to the next place. Ending up in the room of your choice.

2. Meet your partner at the door from a long day's work with nothing on but a Bra, panties, garter belt, stockings, & a pair of C.F.M.P.'S. (High Heels)

3. Candle light dinner with a glass of wine, champagne, or sparkling cider with soft jazz playing in back ground.

4. Send a bouquet of flowers, just because.

5. Leave a note on your partner's pillow.

6. Leave a single rose on your partner's pillow.

7. Give each other a massage. (full body)

8. Give your partner a gift certificate to a spa for pedicure, manicure, massage, or facial.

9. Draw a hot bath for your partner after a long day at work. Turn down or better yet, turn off the lights. Light some candles and put on some soft music. Join your partner in the tub, or feed your partner strawberries covered in chocolate and a glass of your partner's favorite beverage.

10. If your partner travels, place a card or note in his or her suitcase telling him / her how much he / she is missed and you can't wait until they get home.

11. If he or she goes away for a convention and you can take a couple of days off. Go join them.

12. Go away for the weekend even if it's across town. Stay in a 3* hotel or better, remove yourself from the comforts of home.

13. Plan a picnic lunch or dinner complete with blanket. Place down in the middle of the floor either at home in front of a fireplace or at the office. Put a CD in and enjoy your meal.

14. Serve your partner breakfast in bed along with other things.

15. If your spouse goes away meet him or her with a sign at airport saying: Looking for (your spouse's name) Hugs and Kisses waiting.

16. Serve your spouse coffee in bed.

17. Placing a card or note on your partner's pillow, welcoming him or her home from their business trip.

18. Rent a movie that you both like, pop some popcorn and watch it together.

19. Sit in front of a fire with your partner with a mug of hot chocolate or some wine and cheese and reminisce about when you first met, your first kiss, your first touch.

20. Draw a bubble bath and bathe your partner afterwards. Rub lotion on your partner don't forget to massage the feet.

21. If you have children, hire a babysitter and go dancing.

22. Go on a date at least once a month. Even if it means one of you go to a friend's house to get dressed and the other comes to pick you up. Although you will end up at home at the end of the date.

23. Take your partner on a shopping spree at his or her favorite store or Lingerie shop.

24. Go for an evening stroll through the neighborhood and talk about your day.

25. RESPECT your partner!!

26. Tell your partner you love him or her every day and how much you appreciate them. REMEMBER, tomorrow is not promised.

27. Surprise her by ironing her clothes.

28. Make Love to your partner on a pool table.

29. Never go to bed angry.

30. Fill the bath tub with Champagne or Jell-O and join your partner for a late-night snack.

31. If you take your partner on Vacation, don't forget the natural areas to show your appreciation. (the ocean late at night, or in the natural water falls)

32. Don't forget the late night swim at the hotel pool.

33. For those of you who dare to be adventurous. How about making love while going through the car wash.

24. If you cannot get away for the weekend and your partner likes camping why not set the back yard up complete with a tent, & outdoor fire.

35. Remember to always keep the lines of communication open.

36. Ask your partner how was his/her day and actually listen to what he/she has to say. Don't focus on yourself. Remember you asked the question.

37. If you have children plan a surprise lunch for your partner. Let the children help plan, cook, serve and clean-up.

38. Fix a dish and arrange it suggestively, hopefully they will get the hint.

39. On a late night flight when everyone is asleep, join the mile high club. (Be careful not to get caught)

40. Take your partner on a romantic getaway for the weekend.

41. Plan a workout session at the gym with your mate at least once a week. The more the better.

42. Get a manicure and pedicure together.

43. Give your partner a good hug, just because!

44. Pray and worship together.

Notes

INDEX

SPICE IT UP

Recipes with a Sensual Twist

Videos: You tube search: MsLaJuan2
Look forward to more Spice It Up books in the future,

Spice It Up, Cooking lessons 101
Spice It Up, Cooking with the Children
Spice It Up, Fit to Be Tied
Spice It Up, Pleasing Your Palate
Spice It Up, Friends and Family
Spice It Up, Holidays and Seasons